Stefan Spath

111 places
in Salzburg,
that you shouldn't
miss

With Photographs by Pia Odorizzi

GW00467526

emons:

Acknowledgements

Detailed research can sometimes get out of hand and become a Sisyphean task. Which is why I'd like to share a surprising discovery from Salzburg. Rarely have I encountered so many committed civil servants who shared their knowledge with such good grace and enthusiasm. I would like to thank Salzburg Tourism (Tourismus Salzburg GmbH) too, for arranging the contacts and insider information that made this book what it is. I am particularly indebted to my long-term Salzburg friend from our student days, Herbert Moser, who supported me so energetically in my research and in writing texts on selected destinations.

Bibliographical information of the Deutsche Nationalbibliothek
The Deutsche Nationalbibliothek lists this publication
in the Deutsche Nationalbibliografie; detailed bibliographical
data are available on the internet at http://dnb.d-nb.de.

© Hermann-Josef Emons Verlag
All rights reserved
Design: Eva Kraskes, based on a design
by Lübbeke | Naumann | Thoben
Maps: altancicek.design, www.altancicek.de
English translation: Kathleen Becker
Printing and binding: B.O.S.S Druck und Medien GmbH, Goch
Printed in Germany 2013
ISBN 978-3-95451-230-0
First edition

For the latest information about emons, read our regular newsletter:
order it free of charge at www.emons-verlag.de

Foreword

To find 111 unusual places in a city of 1.5 million inhabitants may be an easier feat than for a city of 150,000. Salzburg is a small city, smaller at least than its status as Festival city or World Heritage site might suggest. And even when the research net was widened to include its surroundings, I was initially a little sceptical.

Yet, all of a sudden, a vast number of unusual destinations and stories began tumbling out of this small-town bag of tricks. Where, if not in Salzburg, can you wander a subterranean system of mining shafts, which is still used for its original purpose? Where else will you meet free-roaming city chamois and flamingoes? Where else can you hear the sound of a bell that would have called 15th-century revellers to order? What is a 'pichery' when it's at home, and why would a national border run deep inside a mountain? This book will even take readers familiar with the city to places that will inspire them.

Since my last Salzburg research, so much has changed that I couldn't quite get my head around it all. A surf wave along the Almkanal, architectural surprises in Itzling and Lehen, the city hall all spruced up with its tower full of stories, the miraculous new roof of the Rock Riding School, the completely renovated train station with eye-catching tiles from 1909, or the house of beer culture in Obertrum. All of this – and with no claims to completeness – could be explored by somebody who hadn't visited the banks of the Salzach for a couple of years or who hadn't got under the surface of this place. Take a look at Salzburg's sound art installations, for instance; and even the Augustiner Bräu surprises with unusual features.

If you feel like discovering Salzburg with a new pair of eyes as it were, take heart and enjoy your travels. And one more tip: if you're planning to get a lot of sightseeing under your belt, the Salzburg Card is your ticket to ride.

111 Places

1_ The Marble Quarry
Mecca of red marble

For those in the know, »Adnet Marble« is synonymous with »stone of the highest quality«. Strolling through the town on the Salzach River, it is easy to see how the quarries of Adnet – there used to be 15 of them – delivered the finest building material to nearby Salzburg for centuries. However, Adnet Marble, in particular the red-chequered »Rot-Scheck«, was sold abroad too, as evidenced by the stone carvings of the bishops in Würzburg Cathedral or the *Mariensäule* (Marian column) in Munich.

Geologists call the Adnet quarry zone the »Mecca of red marble« because nowhere else can boast so many different types of marble in such a small space. Alongside the red-chequered marble you can also find coral marble. Usually light in colour, this can also have a reddish-green shimmer to it. The marble museum in the municipal offices is worth a visit, with its overview of the stone quarrying here, presumably started by the Romans back in the 2nd century AD, although the first written evidence we have dates from the year 1420.

The circular hiking trail through the quarrying zone, starting at the museum and lasting some two hours, illustrates marble quarrying past and present. Some quarries are still used to this day for extracting the red-chequered marble. The blocks, up to ten metres/33 feet high, are cut out of the wall using a diamond rope cutter. It takes between three and four days to work a wall. At the Rotgrauschnollbruch quarry you will learn how, in the second half of the 19th century, the rough-hewn slabs for the pillars of the Austrian parliament were cut and prepared here.

These works-of-art-in-waiting, measuring 18 metres/nearly 60 feet, were subsequently transported by horse-drawn cart to Hallein and on to Vienna. At the *Wimbergbruch* quarry you'll encounter a geological phenomenon: red marble on top, with white marble in the layer below.

Address Point of departure Gemeindeamt (municipal offices), Adnet 18, A-5421 Adnet, tel. +43 (0)6245 / 84041, http://marmormuseum.adnet.at | **Opening times** 15 April–26 Oct Tue 9–11am, Thu 3–5pm, Sat 3–5pm | **Access** Aigner Strasse (L 105) or the Alpenstrasse (B 150) and A 10 south, exit 16-Hallein, via L 107 and L 144 into the centre of Adnet | **Tip** The former blacksmith's right in the forest has been converted into a small museum revealing the workings of the »plug-and-feather method« (the oldest technique in stone quarrying).

2__ The People's Observatory
Salzburg's gateway to space

When people hear 'observatory', they think of a tower-like building with one of those characteristic domes opening like a shell and allowing a telescopic glimpse into the depths of space. But Voggenberg's »Volkssternwarte« turns out to be a wooden building on the edge of a country lane.

If you weren't greeted by the impressive model of the solar system – built to a 1:870 million scale – with its wooden model sun mounted on a tree trunk amid a colourful gaggle of planets, you'd never in a million light years suspect that this sober façade hides a powerful observatory.

Of course, this is a fallacy: astronomers find good cosmic vibes in dark and remote places. And the Voggenberg at Bergheim, in the back of beyond really, offers near-perfect conditions. Light pollution from Salzburg, eight km/five miles away, is limited. When the sky is clear, the roof opens, and the main instrument, a Celestron 14 reflector telescope with a focal length of four metres/13 feet and an aperture measuring 35 centimetres/12 inches across, is put into position.

Direct observation through the telescope – long since the exception for stargazers – usually gives visitors an attack of star fever. Eclipses, comets, planets and faraway galaxies can all be seen. When extraordinary sky phenomena are announced, up to 300 curious stargazers make the pilgrimage to Voggenberg.

The observatory attached to the 'Haus der Natur' nature interpretation centre in Salzburg is the only publicly accessible observatory for many miles around. The volunteers working here see the passing on of astronomical knowledge and astrophotography as their main vocation.

Time and again Salzburg's stargazers take part in astronomy programmes where a maximum number of observation points is a definite advantage

Address Salzburger Volkssternwarte, Voggenberg 18 (near Landgasthaus Windinggut country hotel), A-5101 Bergheim, http://astronomie.hausdernatur.at | **Opening times** Guided tours with stargazing every Thu on clear nights Oct−March 8pm, April and Sept 9pm, May, July, Aug 10pm, June 10.30pm | **Access** Via B 156 Lamprechtshausener Strasse, turn right at Furtmuhlstrasse, via Voggenbergstrasse and Korbweg into the hamlet of Voggenberg, on via Windingstrasse to the Winding country hotel. The observatory is situated some 50 metres/ 55 yards along a country lane | **Tip** Only a few yards away, Ragging Lake and Luging Lake are worth exploring on a little hike.

3__ The Glasenbach Gorge

Walking back 200 million years

Shells, remains of corals and plenty of other fossils: the Glasenbach gorge at Elsbethen is testimony to a time when the area around what today is Salzburg was covered by masses of water. It also offers the rare opportunity to travel a good 200 million years back into the past, over a stretch of just three kilometres/1.8 miles! When hiking through the gorge-like valley of the Klausenbach River it pays to keep your eyes open. To this day, heavy rain and erosion on the slopes keep bringing to the surface the remains of living creatures big and small.

The most spectacular find to date happened some 100 years ago, when the teeth, ribs and vertebrae of ichthyosaurs were discovered. Today, the remains of the saurians that once hunted here in the pre-historic seas can be admired in Salzburg's »Haus der Natur« natural history museum.

The metamorphosis from sea floor to mountain landscape is de-scribed by a geology trail along eleven stops. You have to wait for panel no. 10 for the most striking point, where layers, one on top of another and pressed into the most bizarre shapes over the course of millions of years, have created a wave-like pattern on a steep rock wall. The Klamm is characterised by little sunshine, a high degree of humidity and mild temperatures, good not only for mosses, ferns and lichens, but also hikers on a hot summer's day. And in winter, when temperatures plummet, nature creates splendid sculptures of ice and snow.

It's only a short walk to the Trockene Klammen – literally 'dry gorges' – and their bizarre boulders. Hikers with stamina can carry on and climb up to the Erentrudisalm alpine meadow, although stur-dy footwear is a must here.

Schedule at least four hours for the return trip, and you will be richly rewarded with magnificent panoramic views and a typical Salzburg hostelry.

Address Lohhauslweg, A-5061 Elsbethen | Public transport Obus no. 7, stop Glasenbach, approx. 10 minutes on foot or S-Bahn, stop Elsbethen, plus 10 minutes' on foot | Access From Salzburg via Aigner Strasse / L 105; in Elsbethen bear left into Lohhauslweg | Tip From Hinterwinkl at the end of the Glasenbach Gorge, it's not even two kilometres / a good mile to the Egel Lakes, beautiful quiet marshlands in the heart of the forest.

4_ The Marble Mills

Marble balls from the Untersberg – a big hit abroad

It's well-known that marble from Untersberg was once an important export commodity for Salzburg. However, the Untersbergmuseum in Furstenbrunn illustrates one aspect of marble history that has been somewhat forgotten: the marble balls were once a big hit abroad. They came from the marble mills, of which there were dozens around the Untersberg mountain massif.

One of these mills has been revitalised to help visitors understand this traditional craft.

Marble mills started being a lucrative business 300 years ago. Investment costs were low, with the raw material collected in stone quarries or from watercourses.

The mills would produce sought-after spheres in the era of sailing ships, where they served both as ballast and also for filling cannons. One shipload of Untersberg »schussers«, as the smallest of them were called, could shred a sail to bits.

And last but not least, the marbles were also sold for a profit as toys. Documents reveal that in the year 1787, for instance, over 1,000 hundredweight, or 50,000 kilogrammes, of marble balls were exported – that is over ten million marbles. Shipped from Bremen, London and Amsterdam, they would roll their way to the Caribbean and Asia in the bellies of sailing ships.

Exactly how this craft functioned is demonstrated in a marble mill next to the museum. At first the miller forms a piece of marble into an approximately round shape, using a bush hammer or saw. The roughly worked stones are placed into the crushing mill, which is powered by water. It takes between one and three days for the lumps to be polished into a round shape. In their finished and polished state, they are then put on sale in the museum. Their patterns and colours make the fist-sized balls of Untersberg marble a handsome souvenir.

Address Untersbergmuseum, Kugelmühlweg 4, A-5082 Grödig (Fürstenbrunn), tel. +43 (0)6246/72106, http://museum.untersberg.net | Opening times May–Oct Sat, Sun and public holidays 1–6pm; March, April, Nov, Dec Sat, Sun and public holidays 1–5pm; closed Jan, Feb | Public transport Bus no. 21 from Mirabellplatz, last stop Fürstenbrunn Buskehre | Access A 10, exit 8 (Salzburg-Süd), follow signs to Grödig town centre (Zentrum), continue via the L237 (Glaneggerstrasse/Fürstenbrunnerstrasse) to the end of Fürstenbrunn, car park at the museum | Tip The museum dedicates a separate space to the rich folklore surrounding Untersberg. Don't miss the magnificent »Wild Hunt« masks.

5___The Natural Burial Sites

Meadows, trees and alpine pasture as last resting places

The »Dürre Wiese« – which roughly translates as »Barren Meadow« – lies at the foot of the Untersberg mountain massif, near the open-air museum in Großgmain. Contrary to what the name might suggest, this meadow is replete with lush grasses and flowers, with butterflies fluttering from blossom to blossom.

The green space borders a light mixed forest, with a sign the only clue to the fact that people choose the Dürre Wiese to be their final resting place.

In contrast to neighbouring Germany and Switzerland, the Austrian federal state of Salzburg only started permitting natural burials a few years ago. Pioneers in the sector, the paxnatura company offers this kind of burial in three natural spaces on the Untersberg.

The Dürre Wiese is a forest clearing in a perfectly idyllic location. Easier to access is the Kastanienwiese, or »Chestnut Meadow«, just a few hundred yards from the company headquarters in the estate in Glanegg and yet far enough from the street that you might spot the occasional deer between Kastanienallee and Hangwald. The views from here range all the way to Hohensalzburg Castle. Those who prefer the idea of being buried high up the mountain when their time comes, with panoramic views right into Bavaria, can book their final resting place on the Vierkaseralm alpine pasture.

A natural burial involves placing the ashes of the deceased into a biodegradable urn buried at a depth of 70 centimetres/27 inches. The grass turf soon provides a firm cover again. The exact location of the ashes is recorded on a site map. No monuments, crosses or ornaments, with the exception of flowers, are allowed on the natural burial sites.

Only simple plaques on a memorial stone indicate who is resting here. The stone bears the names of the dead with their dates of birth and death. The grave is looked after by nature, according to the seasons.

Address paxnatura Naturbestattungs GmbH, Glanegg 2, A-5082 Grodig, tel. +43 (0)6246/73541, www.paxnatura.at | Public transport bus no. 21 from Mirabellplatz, stop Glanegg Schloss | Access A 10, exit 8 (Salzburg-Sud/south), follow signs to Grodig town centre and continue via Glaneggerstrasse L 237 to Glanegg, car park at the estate | Tip Experienced hikers can climb up to the Geiereck peak from Glanegg using trail no. 417 or 460. However, the easier option is the cable car running from the St Leonhard part of Grodig town up to the Untersberg.

6 The Butterfly Trail
The »butterfly effect« in miniature

The northwestern foot of the Untersberg massif boasts a variety of butterflies that is remarkable within Europe. Seventy of the 150 species of diurnal butterfly that occur in the Salzburg region flutter through this area, characterized by small forests and meadows. In order to preserve this biodiversity, which has come under pressure, Salzburg's open-air museum and surroundings run a LIFE Nature project sponsored by the EU and have it explained by the butterfly experience trail.

Above all, it is changes in farming that have brought about a »butterfly effect«. Heavy fertilisation, as well as early and frequent cutting of the meadows, results in fewer blossoms forming, which in turn deprives the butterflies of their food source.

In the area of the open-air museum, however, conditions for these sensitive insects have been optimised. Alongside the all-important wetland meadows with their sources of nectar, there are clearings – transition areas between field and forest – alongside specifically created biotopes, which offer ideal habitat conditions for these creatures.

Trees have been planted specifically for the rare and beautiful Scarce Fritillary, which will only lay its eggs on ash trees. Another butterfly dependent on a specific species of plant is the rare Alcon Blue. Here it finds the marsh gentian where it can deposit its eggs, and which then serve as food for the larvae.

These connections are explained to visitors using display panels, a butterfly quiz and a documentary. There is also an observation tower, from which you can catch a glimpse of this butterfly paradise. However, in order to spy the graceful stars of the Untersberg fauna in their dance from flower to flower, you'll need a slice of luck, perhaps some binoculars, and definitely patience. The best chance is on sunny days with little wind.

...rland – Teil des europäischen Natu...

...s natural heritage

Richtung Salzburg

438

Zollamt

Kuglstätter

Wartberg

Meister

542

Wartberg

Schmörzh

SALZBURG

516

Schmetterling in Not

Der Eschen-Scheckenfalter (Euphyc...

dass er europaweit und ... Schutz ste...

Address Salzburger Freilichtmuseum, Hasenweg, A-5084 Großgmain, tel. +43 (0)662/ 850011, www.freilichtmuseum.com | Opening times Late March–June Tue–Sun 9am–6pm; July, Aug daily 9am–6pm; Sept–early Nov Tue–Sun 9am–6pm (from early Oct onwards only to 5pm) | Public transport Regional bus no. 180 (direction Bad Reichenhall) from Salzburg Hauptbahnhof main station, stop Großgmain Freilicht-museum | Access Via A1, exit Salzburg-West or Wals/exit 297, then via B1 and L114 some 5 kilometres/3 miles to the open-air museum (look out for signposts) | Tip Binoculars come in handy for butterfly spotting. A rustic alpine snack, aromatic cheese gnocchi and other regional specialities served in the Gasthaus Salettl hostelry round off any visit to the open-air museum.

7_ The Narrow-Gauge Railway Museum

On narrow tracks to old farmsteads

With its magnificent farmsteads and engaging demonstrations of traditional, rural ways of working, Salzburg's open-air museum draws many visitors. However, the agrarian exhibition has been enriched by a fascinating chapter of transport history: a museum train trundling through the extensive area at a top speed of 15 kilometres/9 miles per hour makes the rich tradition of Salzburg's narrow-gauge trains come alive again.

Narrow-gauge railways linking fields, forests, industrial or construction sites were used where limitations of terrain or financial expenditure didn't allow transport by traditional goods train or truck. With turf-cutting in Burmoos, for instance, the boggy ground would only support a train of small dimensions, while during construction of the Grossglockner high alpine road in the 1930s, and of the Glockner-Kaprun group of power stations, the excavated material was carted off by narrow-gauge train. The historical spread of these miniature trains in the Salzburg region is shown by an exhibition in the »Bahnhof Flachgau« railway station, where the museum train starts its journey. Die-hard railway fans will be thrilled by the fact that the building represents a reconstruction of a stop on the route of the rack-and-pinion train which puffed its ways up to Salzburg's Gaisberg between 1887 and 1928.

The route network comprises 1,700 metres/over a mile, as well as three stops with turning loops at the end ones. Locomotives and carriages were collected from all over Europe and adapted for use on this stretch, which involves a 4% gradient. One of the museum railway's locomotives was previously used in the construction of the Channel Tunnel, and another was taken over from the Diabaswerk in Saalfelden, which until 2008 boasted the last working narrow-gauge train in Salzburg.

Address Salzburger Freilichtmuseum (open-air museum), Hasenweg, A-5084 Großgmain, tel. +43 (0)662/850011, www.freilichtmuseum.com | **Opening times** late March – June Tue – Sun 9am – 6pm; July, Aug daily 9am – 6pm; Sept – early Nov Tue – Sun 9am – 6pm (from early Oct only to 5pm) | **Public transport** Regional bus no. 180 (direction of Bad Reichenhall) every hour from Salzburg main train station, stop Großgmain Freilichtmuseum | **Access** via A 1, exit Salzburg-West or Wals / exit 297, after that via B 1 and L 114 approx. 5 kilometres/3 miles to the open-air museum (watch out for signposts) | **Tip** Museum visitors with an eye for detail should check out the mousetrap exhibition in the Anthofer Getreidekasten (Hofensemble Lungau).

8__ The Celtic Museum
A high culture still surrounded by question marks

Druidic rituals and witchcraft, tree horoscopes and cult sites: over the past few decades, the Celts have become a general reference point for New Age followers. However, for those who want to find out more about these mysterious tribal groups there is no better place than the Celtic Museum in Hallein.

The basis of the collection is formed by the precious burial findings at Dürrnberg mountain, where, from about 550 BC up to the advance of the Romans, the tribes maintained an economic and political hub based on salt extraction, which radiated far into Central Europe.

The »white gold« trade made the Dürrnberg salt lords wealthy and triggered an unprecedented cultural explosion. The extraordinary skills of the Celtic craftsmen are exemplified by the world-famous beak-spouted jug from the La Tene era (5th – 1st century BC), the original of which can now once again be admired in the Celtic Museum, and a reconstructed chariot, amongst others.

However, the detail here is equally fascinating. Remains of tissue salvaged from the salt works, with a density of 32 threads per square centimetre and a thread thickness of 0.1 millimetre are evidence of highly advanced weaving art. The Celts also mastered various techniques of fabric dying, and developed water-repellent hats from birch bark.

Another extraordinary feature is the variety of forms used in clasps. We have one of the 1,300 found objects to thank for the knowledge that the Celts wore tapered shoes.

Other burial finds include jewellery such as coloured and ornately decorated glass bracelets, for which it's still not clear exactly how they were made. That the Celts put great store by personal hygiene is evidenced by findings of toiletry sets. Their dead would have started the life beyond equipped with tweezers, nail clippers and little ear picks.

Address Pflegerplatz 5, A-5400 Hallein, tel. +43 (0)6245/80783, www.keltenmuseum.at and www.kelten.co.at | Opening times daily 9am–5pm | Public transport S3 to Hallein, 10 minutes on foot in the direction of Salzach, across the bridge, turning right into Kuffergasse | Access A10, exit 16-Hall | Tip Why not carry on learning in Durrnberg's faithfully reconstructed Celtic village (at the salines)? In summer they put on attractive activities for all the family.

9__ The International Border – below ground

The miners managed to burrow deep into Bavaria

»State border Republic of Austria–Federal Republic of Germany« is what it says on the sign deep inside the show mine. Visitors descending into the salty worlds of Hallein might expect miner's slides and attacks of claustrophobia. But a border marker 80 metres/262 feet below the ground? So did the miners of Salzburg dig deep to enter Bavarian territories and steal the salt?

The answer has to do with a historical deal of the »salt for wood« type. The former was a scarce commodity in medicval times for the Durrnberg miners under the control of the Salzburg archbishops, while the latter was scarce for their rivals from the Reichenhall Salines, belonging to the Fürstpropstei Berchtesgaden – an independent territory, later part of Bavaria.

So it was that in the year 1217 the regional rulers of the time agreed on an exchange: the Salzburgians were given the right to tap the underground salt deposits beyond the border, while their rivals were granted the right to cut wood in Salzburg's Pinzgau area to fire Reichenhall's breweries, »in perpetuity«. This marked the birth of an odd curiosity, which remained in place despite all neighbourly animosities between Bavaria and Salzburg and was once again reconfirmed in 1957.

Today, the Saline Convention represents the oldest national treaty in Europe still in force. Since the end of salt mining on Dürrnberg in 1989, it's mainly visitors to the mine who are involved in this small-scale German-Austrian border traffic. To this end, the entire range of mining transport is used, from the shaft train to the miners' slide. The highlight has got to be the underground rafting trip across a salt lake, illuminated to full effect. Visitors emerge into the light of day in the Salzburg area. No passport is needed for this trip on the trail of the »white gold«.

Address Salzwelten Hallein, Ramsaustraße 3, A-5422 Hallein (Bad Durrnberg), tel. +43 (0)6132/2008511, www.salzwelten.at | Opening times Late March–early Nov 9am–5pm, early Nov–early Jan and end of Jan–end of March 10am–3pm | Public transport From Hallein train station (S3 ab Salzburg), a post bus commutes every hour to the salt mine in Bad Durrnberg. | Access A10, exit 16-Hallein, follow signs for the town centre (Zentrum); on via B159 and Durrnberg-Landesstrasse | Tip Don't forget to bring warm clothing! Located above the salt world, the pilgrimage church of Mariae Himmelfahrt, erected around 1600 and dedicated to the Assumption of the Virgin Mary, exudes baroque flair.

10__ The Preacher's Chair

Where Protestants held secret services

A moss-covered rock in the middle of the forest is not usually a place where history is written. Things are different in the Abtswald – which translates as 'Abbot's Forest' – on Hallein's Dürrnberg, which shelters an important monument to Salzburg's ecclesiastical history in the shape of the »Preacher's Chair«. Over 300 years ago, a Protestant activist by the name of Joseph Schaitberger would use this elevated spot to hold prayer sessions for the mountain miners of Dürrnberg. That these were secretly Protestant was well-known to the arch-Catholic rulers of Salzburg.

Until that point it had been tolerated, as the miners played a key role in the economy of the country. Yet these open-air sermons seemed to be the final straw. When all exhortations to recant proved fruitless, the Catholic authorities expelled Schaitberger in 1686, increasing pressure on the Protestants. When they didn't get anywhere with his adherents, the first expulsion orders were issued. And when archbishop Firmian took office, the rabble-rousers won the day in Salzburg. In 1730, the ruler of the region ordered anybody who refused to explicitly convert to the Catholic faith to be expelled with immediate effect.

Salzburg was to lose 20,000 people, a fifth of its population, through the exodus of Protestants that followed. At Dürrnberg, the miners had resigned themselves to their fate. Stirred on by the prospect of freedom of religion the departure didn't weigh too heavily on their minds.

It is said that 780 people cleared their houses in 1732 and descended the mountain to Hallein to board boats taking them to Regensburg. The whole thing is said to have happened »very peacefull and modestlee«, as a chronicle of the time tells us. The exiled Protestants were to find new homes in Prussia, the Netherlands and in the US state of Georgia. For Salzburg, their exodus brought about an economic downturn.

Address Abtswald, Protestantenweg, A-5422 Hallein (Bad Durrnberg) | Access A 10, exit 16-Hallein, follow signs to the town centre (Zentrum); via B 159 and Dürrnberg-Landesstrasse to Zinkenlift (or take the post bus), on via the Raspenhohenweg to the Abtswald-Forstweg barriers; the preacher's chair can be reached by a good 25-minute walk | Tip From the preacher's chair, a short hike leads onto the Truckenthannalm high alpine pasture for a wonderful nature experience.

11 __ The Silent Night Museum
The most important guitar in musical history?

What do you think is the most important guitar in the history of music? The electronic beast that Jimi Hendrix set fire to with lighter fuel on 31 March 1967 in London's Astoria Theatre, shocking the world and public opinion? The one that Pete Townshend destroyed by mistake during one of the first »The Who« gigs in 1964, from which he went on to develop smashing guitars into an art form? The one used by Elvis Presley to perfect his hip sway? Or maybe this modest instrument on display in a glass case in the Silent Night Museum in Hallein?

It might look tired – the strings and pins are no longer the original ones, and some of the inlay is broken. But this is the very guitar that Joseph Mohr used to accompany his poem »Silent Night, Holy Night« for the first time after Mass on Christmas Eve 1818 in St. Nicolaus Church in Oberndorf to a melody by the composer Franz Xaver Gruber – because the organ had given up the ghost. At the time, the guitar was considered an instrument of the people. And the young priest Mohr felt connected to the common people himself, not owning much more than the clothes he stood up in – and the guitar.

Following Franz Xaver Gruber's death in 1848 the guitar was auctioned off, and, via a circuitous route, ended up in 1911 with Gruber's grandson, whose collection was to provide the base for Hallein's Silent Night Museum in the former living quarters of Mohr's partner. Original furniture, writing implements, a pocket watch and many other small items from the composer's possessions can be seen here. Documents tell the story of the emergence and spread of the famous song, but the undisputed star of the museum is the guitar. Hendrix, The Who and Elvis might have sold millions of records, but what is all that compared to a song that an estimated two billion people will intone every Christmas, and that has been translated into 300 languages and dialects?

Address Gruberplatz 1, A-5400 Hallein, tel. +43 (0)6245/85394 (Hallein Tourism Association), www.stillenachthallein.at | Opening times 7 Jan–1st Advent Sunday daily 3–5pm; 1st Advent–6 Jan daily 11am–5pm, 24 Dec 11am–2pm | Public transport From the station across the Salzach into the Old Town, some 15 mins on foot | Access A10, exit 16-Hallein, follow signposts for the town centre (Zentrum); alternatively via Aigner Strasse/L105 to Hallein | Tip Hallein's Old Town is a gem, with many corners providing reminders of the town's salt mining tradition.

12 — The Aiderbichl Farm

Where the animals just love life

Those visiting Gut Aiderbichl will soon stop wondering about un-usual encounters. A peacock strutting his stuff here, a donkey greet-ing visitors over there. Ponies and mules cavort around this unusual farmstead at Henndorf on Lake Waller. Even llamas make a cameo appearance here. The idea of founder Michael Aufhauser when opening the farmstead in 2001 was to enable animals that have suf-fered a lot to spend the rest of their days in a positive way. Gut Aider-bichl has since become something of an institution. Raising public awareness brought about donations and prominent VIP supporters such as much-loved actor Uschi Glas and TV presenter Thomas Gott-schalk. Today, some 3,800 animals are able to lead a dignified exis-tence on some 20 estates and farms under the auspices of Gut Aider-bichl.

The »original« Aiderbichl Estate has had many touching animal stories. Lilli the calf, for instance, was born in Switzerland with six legs. Gut Aiderbichl organised an operation, and Lilli has since en-joyed a carefree life on the hills above Lake Waller. As has Pinot Gri-gio, a successful dressage horse until a heart problem ended his sport-ing career. Or take the bull that wouldn't grow to full size and was given the name Lilliput. Mobbed by his peers, he was placed in a pen with a few amicable cows who were past calf-bearing age – or so it was assumed until one day Sylvia the cow trotted across the pasture visibly pregnant. People are still trying to figure out how these two managed the »miracle« of procreating Amarillo.

By the way, the satellite operation of Aiderbichl in Deggendorf in Bavaria is home to the famous cow Yvonne, who became a dar-ling of the popular press in 2011 following a flight from the butch-er's knife lasting weeks. In 2012, Yvonne was dragged in front of the TV cameras as the oracle for football's European Championships, but turned out to be of little use there, presumably as she was too re-laxed.

Address Berg 20, A-5302 Henndorf am Wallersee, tel. +43 (0)662/625395113, www.gut-aiderbichl.com | Opening times daily 9am–6pm | Public transport Post bus no. 130 from Salzburg main train station, stop Gersbach, by shuttle service on to the estate | Access A1 Richtung Linz/Wien (Vienna), take exit 281-Wallersee in the direction of B1/Eugendorf then follow the B1 to the exit Wiener Strasse, turn right onto Henndorfer Landesstrasse/L 241, then follow signs to Gut Aiderbichl | Tip Two fine destinations for a trip into the surrounding area are the ruined castle of Lichtentann some two km/1.5 miles to the northeast and, a little more difficult to get to, the Grosse Plaike peak with its fabulous panoramic views.

13__ The Wiesmühle Farm

Paradise for the literary great Carl Zuckmayer

Home-smoked streaky bacon, a double shot of clear fruit brandy, a cold beer in a tin-lidded 'Seidl' (a jug containing a third of a litre), a chunk of Mondsee cheese – this is how the German writer Carl Zuckmayer (1896–1977) liked to reward himself in the Caspar-Moser-Bräu hostelry in Henndorf after the literary work of the day was done or after a hike onto the Zifanken peak.

The author of successful literary works such as »The Devil's General« was the key figure of a literary circle which found its Shangri-La between the wars at Lake Waller – this is how Zuckmayer was to describe it in his »Henndorfer Pastorale« and in his autobiography »A Part of Myself, Portrait of an Epoch«. In 1938, when the Nazis seized power in Austria too, Zuckmayer was forced to leave his adopted homeland.

It is worth going on the trail of the spirit of this self-contained landscape with its hills and softly rolling fields, which provided literary inspiration not only to Carl Zuckmayer. Erich Maria Remarque and Marlene Dietrich would visit, while Odon von Horvath wrote parts of his seminal novel »Youth without God« in the Caspar-Moser-Bräu, where he occupied the so-called Ghost Room. Armed with the »A Literary Walk« brochure published by the local authorities, you can explore the most important locations on Lake Waller by bike or on foot.

Purchased by Zuckmayer in 1926, the farm was to become his true paradise. In private hands now, the Wiesmühle can only be visited by literary tourists as part of a guided tour. The items on view include the imposing tiled stove kindly donated by Stefan Zweig, author of the influential »Royal Game« novella amongst many other works, and the garden bench where Zuckmayer would put his ideas to paper.

Those wanting to stay for longer can rent a room in the hunting lodge that forms part of the Wiesmühle, and enjoy the hearty »Original Zuckmayer-Jause« supper served in style today in the Stelzhamer Stube hostelry.

Address Carl Zuckmayerweg 23, A-5302 Henndorf, tel. +43 (0)6214/8303,
www.wiesmuehl.at, Accommodation in the hunting lodge next door | Opening times
only as part of a guided tour, bookable through literaturhaus-henndorf@aon.at | Public
transport Post bus no. 130 from Salzburg main train station, stop Henndorf/Gemeinde-
amt | Access Take the A 1 Richtung Linz/Wien, take exit 281-Wallersee in the direction
of B 1/Eugendorf and follow the federal road into the centre of Henndorf, turning left into
Carl Zuckmayerweg past the municipal offices (Gemeindeamt) | Tip Opened in December
2012, the Literaturhaus below the parish church presents the work of Zuckmayer and of
less well-known authors with a connection to Henndorf.

14___ The Leopold Kohr Show
Yesterday's ideas for a better tomorrow

»Small is beautiful« – everyone knows this slogan, used in the most diverse of contexts. However, few people know the origin of the saying.

In fact, the trail leads to Oberndorf near Salzburg. A miniature exhibition, inside the museum dedicated to the Silent Night hymn and local history, commemorates a man who chose the praise of everything small as a guiding principle, supporting this theory with many examples and works. His name was Leopold Kohr.

Born and bred in Oberndorf (1909–1994), Kohr led a life that could fill ten: reporting from the Spanish civil war, fighting in the anti-Nazi resistance, prospecting for gold in Canada, advising the Caribbean island state of Anguilla, working as a professor of national economics in Mexico, Puerto Rico and Wales – just to name the most interesting stints! The thread linking his work is fascinating too. Fifty years ago Kohr was already fighting the bloated structures in politics and economics which he considered responsible for the last instance for poverty and degradation of democracy. Multinationals and big banks would be his targets today, as much as European »centralism«; his preference was for advocating small structures, rooted in the regions. Kohr created the famous slogan »small is beautiful« to express his plea for a »human measure« in everything.

Kohr's ideas inspired environmental and civil rights movements around the globe. In 1983, he received the alternative Nobel prize, the »Right Livelihood Award«. These ideas seem more relevant than ever in times of crumbling big banks, bankrupt nation states and an out-of-control financial system. The Leopold Kohr Academy in Oberpinzgau and a research centre at the Uni Salzburg are trying to make his ideas heard. Kohr lies buried in Oberndorf cemetery, and to this day there is no monument to this citizen of the world who dared to think outside the box.

JOHN SEYMOU
LAUDATIO
FÜR
LEOPOLD KOH

Address Stille Nacht und Heimatmuseum Oberndorf, Stille-Nacht-Platz 7, A-5110
Oberndorf near Salzburg, tel. +43 (0)6272 / 4422 | **Opening times** Daily 9am – 4pm,
during Advent (Dec) to 6pm, closed in Feb | **Public transport** Take the Salzburg local
train from Salzburg main train station to Oberndorf main train station (Hauptbahnhof),
then 15 minutes on foot | **Access** From Salzburg take the B 156 north, 3 kilometres /
under 2 miles before getting to Oberndorf turn left onto the B 156a, continue in the
direction of the town centre and follow signs into the Stille Nacht zone on the Salzach
loop | **Tip** Do as Leopold Kohr did and tackle the roughly 20 kilometres / 12 mile stretch
from Salzburg to Oberndorf on the Salzach cycle path.

15__ The Silent Night Chapel
Memorial site hiding a gruesome secret

Oberndorf near Salzburg is famous for being the town where the »Silent Night, Holy Night« Christmas carol was sung for the first time, on 24 December 1818, by the curate Joseph Mohr and the organist Franz Xaver Gruber. Today, a small chapel in the Silent Night area serves as a reminder of the original site of the first performance, the church of St. Nicholas, which was demolished around 1900. The interior is sober, with portraits of the creators of the famous song adorning the fine stained glass windows. Of the tens of thousands of visitors, only a few know that the altar of the chapel harbours a macabre secret: the walled-in skull of Joseph Mohr.

The story goes that around 1910, the idea came up at Mohr's last place of priestly work in Wagrain to honour the lyricist with a monument. However, there was one minor problem: there wasn't a single likeness of Mohr, who had died in 1848 as poor as the proverbial church mouse. Nobody could remember what he looked like. Thus, the sculptor commissioned for the job, priest Joseph Mühlbacher, pressed for an exhumation. After a long search the remains were located in the cemetery of Wagrain, whereupon the sculptor used the skull as »inspiration« for Joseph Mohr's traits on his relief – a polite way of saying he created an imaginary likeness.

However, the people of Wagrain had no money to buy the artwork, and it was only in 1928 that it was completed in an extended form – as the Mohr/Gruber sculpture – and erected at a different spot, in Oberndorf. This was also where the skull had ended up, which seems to have given rise to the idea of walling it into the Silent Night Chapel erected in place of the demolished baroque church (completed in 1936), as a kind of relic. Those who did it kept quiet (no documents can be found pertaining to this), and the people of Wagrain were left to wonder, but the probability is that the skull found his last resting place where the song rang out for the first time.

Address Stille-Nacht-Platz, A-5110 Oberndorf bei Salzburg, www.stillenacht-oberndorf.at | Opening times Daily 8am–6pm | Public transport By Salzburg local train every half hour from Salzburg main train station to Oberndorf station, 15 minutes on foot | Access From Salzburg take the B 156 north, 3 kilometres/under 2 miles before you get to Oberndorf, turn left onto the B 156a in the direction of the town centre and follow the signs to Stille Nacht Bezirk on the Salzach loop | Tip The Gruber/Mohr sculpture by Mühlbach is located in front of the parish church. A circular trail (approx. two to three hours) connects the most interesting attractions of Oberndorf (Austria) and Laufen (Germany) on the opposite sides of the Salzach River.

16__The House of Beer Culture

There's more to hops and malt than meets the eye

Is it just our imagination or does the beer served in a bulging glass at the BierKulturHaus taste spicy, slightly of honey with a trace of … forest aromas? If these are the fruits of Axel Kiesbye's experimentations around the vat of his creative brewery, it can't be just our imagination.

In Obertrum, north of Salzburg, the master brewer, originally from Dortmund in Germany, is tireless in his efforts to bring a greater degree of attention to the 6,000-year old cultural beverage that is beer. Kiesbye's particular interest lies in reviving ingredients today seen as »exotic«, but which in truth have only been forgotten about, and to use their potential to extend the traditional range of flavours of beer. For his »Waldbier« (forest beer) for instance, Kiesbye added the young shoots of fir branches to the brew. And for the Edition 2012 he relied on the aroma of Swiss stone pine cones.

This meeting point for beer lovers is housed on the lower ground floor of a traditional brewery. Here, groups of beer aficionados can produce their own beer in a historical facility made for hand-brewing, under the supervision of a master brewer – stronger or lighter variations, with notes of cassis or herbs perhaps, or more traditional styles. Six to eight weeks later the personal brew is ready for consumption.

In cookery courses and culinary seminars, participants are taught which beer goes best with different types of food – beyond pork roast and rustic cold platter. The first port of call in the house is the Beerotheque where you can taste and buy specialities such as the forest beer, Belgian fruit beers or stouts from Scotland. The tastings make use of the degustation glass developed by Kiesbye. The cellar with its precious vintage beers is worth a look too. And if you still haven't had enough you can even train to acquire the beer sommelier diploma and become an »ambassador« for this cultural beverage.

Address Dorfplatz 1, A-5162 Obertrum am See, tel. +43 (0)664/2807317,
www.bierkulturhaus.com | Opening times on request | Public transport Regional
bus no. 120 from Salzburg main train station, stop Ortsmitte (centre) | Access
From Salzburg take the B 150 and B 156 north and continue via Mattseer Land-
strasse / L 101 to Obertrum, driving in the direction of the town centre, car park
at the Braugasthof Sigl brewery | Tip The guided tours through the Trum private
brewery across the road are highly recommended too. Finish by enjoying panoramic
views across the Trum lakes with a glass of freshly drawn pilsener in your hand.

17 __ The Salzburgring
The ultimate circuit for petrol-heads

To the east of Salzburg, between the parishes of Koppl, Plainfeld and Hof, the Salzburgring race track was opened in 1969 to bring the glamour of Formula 1 to the area. While this particular dream was not fulfilled, a number of Formula 1 idols did climb into the cockpit for Formula 2 races on the Salzburgring: legends such as Graham Hill and Emerson Fittipaldi, as well as racing icon Jochen Rindt, who contested a last race here before his fatal accident six days later training in Monza on 5 September 1970.

Motorbike World Championship races were once very popular with the fans here. Up to 100,000 spectators would descend on the circuit, especially when aces such as Giacomo Agostini and Toni Mang were scheduled to appear. Events of this kind are in the past now though. Since the last motorbike world championship run in 1994, the 4.25km/2.65-mile round circuit is now used for presentations and driving courses of well-known car brands, club meetings and test days. An exception is the touring car world championship run – the season between April and mid-November is always booked up.

Its location in a valley basin provides the course with natural grandstands, providing spectators with great views – from the paddock bend you can keep three quarters of the run in your sights. Motorsports fans who like to take their own vehicles or motorbikes for a spin on a few circuits can book special dates for free driving. Another option is to contact the car companies or clubs who have booked the course, to take part in their drives. One day, star conductor Herbert von Karajan, who also enjoyed the odd test run here, gave rise to an anecdote: He faxed an order of four free VIP tickets for a world championship run to Willy Lowinger, president at the time of the Austrian sports automobile club. Lowinger agreed, on the condition that the maestro would provide four free VIP tickets for the Salzburg Festival, which Karajan was happy to do.

Address Salzburgring 1, A-5325 Plainfeld, www.salzburgring.com | Opening times
April–Nov, bookings for free driving (»Freies Fahren«) under tel. +43 (0)662 / 848734 |
Access From Salzburg take Wolfgangsee-Strasse / B 158 in the direction of Plainfeld,
turn left at Habachstrasse and follow the signs to Salzburgring | Tip The »Manro«
museum in nearby Koppl shows classic vintage cars – from Ferraris, Jaguars, Mercedes
and Maseratis all the way to the Ford A.

18__ The Aigner Park
Life of leisure on historical culture trails

Spending time among nature changes the inner pace of a person. This is something the good people of Salzburg realised 200 years ago. Aigner Park in the southeast of the city, laid out around 1780 in the Enlightenment era on the wooded hills of the Gaisberg, is one of the most important expressions of early 19th century garden architecture.

When Canon Ernst Fürst von Schwarzenberg had the park extended in 1804, pretty recesses, gloriettes, grottoes, hermitages, winding paths, gorges, waterfalls and sublime viewpoints came to adorn this extensive park east of Aigen Castle. Even a health spa was set up, as the Bitterquelle spring had been credited with healing powers since the late Middle Ages.

At the time, Aigner Park was a point of reference for visitors to Salzburg from all over Europe, in the same way that Mozart's birthplace is today. Painters depicted it as paradise, while poets and romantics gushed about a »reflection of heavenly splendour«. King Ludwig I. of Bavaria wrote the following in the guestbook: »Unique you are, comely Aigen, with no equal in the unsurvey'd world«.

Today's visitors, tackling the paths and steps of the steeply rising hill in the direction of the Gaisberg peak, might not quite share this exalted enthusiasm. The Jägerloch (Hunter's Den; lit. »hole«), once a splendid viewpoint, has long been covered in dense trees, and Aigner Park has become a tranquil refuge for seekers of short-term leisure. The aromatic air, refreshing on a hot summer's day, revives the spirits, while benches along the way beckon for a rest.

The lower grotto, which goes by the name of »Hexenloch« (Witches Den), is considered the entrance to a mystical cave. According to a 1792 report, this was the meeting point for the »Illuminati«, a lodge with ties to the Freemasons. These days, Aigner Park is what the Salzburg environmental code calls a »protected part of the landscape«.

Address Schwarzenbergpromenade 37, A-5026 Salzburg (Aigen) | **Opening times** free admission all year round | **Public transport** Obus 7, stop Überfuhrstrasse, then on foot for some 20 minutes | **Tip** Aigen Castle, an old manor of the Salzburg cathedral chapter right in front of the entrance to Aigner Park, houses a cosy hostelry.

19__ The Alp Waves

Good vibrations for Salzburg's surfing subculture

The desire to practice exotic sports on your doorstep can sometimes have surprising consequences – as happened in Salzburg, where a few years ago surf aficionados spotted the chance to realise their dreams of surfboard freedom in the shape of a cascade in the Gneis part of town, along the briskly flowing Alp canal. It took a little lobbying, but they made it happen. In September 2010 the small cascade descending from the alpine meadows was extended by a wooden ramp and a widened channel to form a training spot for surfers and kayakers: the »Almwelle« was born – and became an instant success.

In good weather, more than a dozen surfers stage their balancing contests, and even in late autumn you can still see some of them speeding across the pale blue waters of the canal. Most surfers are equipped with helmet and wetsuit, others just make do with swimming shorts.

Of course, Salzburg's river surfer scene is surfing, as it were, the wave of popularity triggered by the Eisbach in Munich where urban surfing has been a cult activity for 20 years now. However, there are a few differences: two movable spoilers allow for the form of the wave surfing »on the Alp« to be modified. At 0.5 metres/a good 1.5 feet in height and 4.5 metres/15 feet wide, Salzburg's wave is also a fair bit smaller, allowing a maximum of two surfers to ride it simultaneously.

Connoisseurs of the scene will find excellent conditions at this hotspot on the edge of the Alp Canal in which to learn the art of surfing a standing wave. A local pioneer even developed a board tailored for the specifics of the Alp Wave. Despite all this, many a ride ends in the ice-cold water after just a few seconds.

There isn't much infrastructure here to speak of. However, the surfers seem able to live with that, and passers-by enjoy the colourful scene anyway.

Address Heinrich-Meder-Weg, A-5020 Salzburg (Gneis) | Opening times All year round | Public transport Obus 5, last stop Birkensiedlung; from the Obuskehre follow the canal for 150 metres/165 yards towards the town centre | Tip Wetsuits and riverboards may be purchased from Seidl Board & Fashion (Gnigler Straße 35, tel. +43 (0)662/871258, www.boardshop.at). Walking and biking along the Almkanal are great fun too.

20_ The Alpine Milk HQ

The best dairy produce plus award-winning industrial design

In densely populated urban areas, food-production firms don't have an easy time of it: the view of grey industrial façades, noise, air pollution, traffic or a mix of all of these often ensure that the locals, fearing for their quality of life, mount a campaign to stop the company setting up shop. The Alpine Milk headquarters in the Itzling part of town has never had any of these image problems. Housed since 2010 in a new home built from scratch, this is not only a hyper-modern company, but also a model project of contemporary industrial architecture.

And so when you first lay eyes on the building you might ask yourself: is this a museum of modern art or a stranded ocean liner? The reason for the confusion is the façade of aluminium panels and blue tinted windows stretching along the entire street front of the Alpine Milk HQ.

The frontage, designed by Tyrolean artist Peter Sandbichler using untreated aluminium, also signals transparency and raises curiosity. The message is clear: Salzburg's biggest dairy company has nothing to hide. This holds true for hygiene, for instance, which of course is of prime importance in food processing. But visitors will quickly spot what this place is all about from the brightly coloured plastic cows spreading good vibes around the entrance area.

Behind the chic façade – in the second row as it were – is where you'll find everything needed to turn 160 million kilogrammes of milk into 360 different products belonging to the »white line« (milk, yoghurt and curd), the »yellow line« (cheese) and the »coloured line« (mixed dairy products), to pack them and store them until they are transported to the consumer.

The most space is taken up by cold storage, which, protected by the aluminium façade and set back from the street, almost vanishes from view.

Address Alpenmilch Salzburg Ltd, Milchstrasse 1, A-5020 Salzburg (Itzling),
tel. +43 (0)662/24550, www.milch.com | Public transport Local train stop Itzling,
Obus 6, stop Erzherzog-Eugen-Strasse | Tip At the dairy shop (open Monday to
Friday 6.30am to 3pm) anyone can purchase delicacies such as cheeses made with
wild garlic or paprika, by the kilo.

21 The Antretter Private Chapel

Backyard gem

Towers, domes, pinnacles and spires wherever the eye may roam – Salzburg's silhouette is dominated by church towers of all epochs and architectural styles. Some churches however are so special that they have stayed hidden from most curious glances; we are talking about the private chapels of wealthy and distinguished aristocratic families.

One of the last of its kind can be found tucked away in a backyard amidst the hustle and bustle of the Old Town. The door to Mozartplatz Number 4, the »Antretter Haus«, stands open, and a few paces on the passage opens up into a leafy courtyard.

A gem of art history, the Mariae Himmelfahrt house chapel, dedicated to the Assumption of the Virgin Mary, can be spotted at the far end, rising like a miniature version of the major baroque churches. The predominantly yellow chapel is equipped with a small bell tower crowned by an onion dome. Rococo windows structure the front façade, and a Madonna adorns the relief in the tympanum. That, together with a rear view visible from Rudolfskai, will have to do you, as the chapel is in private hands and not open to the public.

The chapel forms part of a former town palace built by the noble dynasty of Rehlingen in the late 16th century. Johann Ernst von Antretter, in his office as »Chancellor of the Province of Salzburg« and Royal War Councillor, purchased the estate in 1765 and had the chapel restored.

The family was good friends with the Mozarts. The daughter, Maria Anna (»Nannerl«), would be given piano lessons by a young Wolfgang Amadeus, who was not only friends with Cajetan, the son of the family, but also composed the famous Antretter Serenade in d major (KV 185) for orchestra in honour of Frau Antretter. So it is very possible that Mozart too would often have been found in this hidden private chapel.

Address Mozartplatz 4, A-5020 Salzburg | **Public transport** Buses no. 3, 5, 6, 7, 8, 20, 25, 28, 160, 170, stop Mozartsteg/Rudolfskai | **Tip** »Salzburg auf neuen Wegen« (Discover Salzburg on new trails) is the title of an inspiring brochure (German only, K TO CHECK) for urban walkers, available free of charge right next door at the Salzburg Information tourist office on Mozartplatz no. 2.

22__ The Balkan Grill

The Bosna: Salzburg's answer to the curried sausage

The year 1949 was an extraordinary year in sausage history. At her snack stall in Berlin-Charlottenburg, a certain Herta Heuwer was the first to garnish a boiled sausage with a spontaneously invented sauce of tomato puree, curry powder and other ingredients – the classic curried sausage, or Currywurst, was born.

At the same time, 600 kilometres/some 380 miles to the south, Bulgarian-born Zanko Todoroff was vying for sausage supremacy in Salzburg. In the Augustinian brewery at Mülln, he set up a stove and fried pork sausages, before placing them in a warmed white roll, with plenty of finely chopped onion.

Todoroff added parsley and a hot spice mix, which was kept secret but did have an obvious curry tendency, and another sausage classic – famed in Salzburg and Upper Austria at least – was born!

There are two theories on exactly how the sausage got the name »Bosna«: the breezy renaming of the Balkan variation on the hotdog is ascribed to customers who couldn't memorise the name Todoroff had originally chosen: »Nadanitza«. Also, it is said, the sausage pioneer himself commissioned a sign for his own stand, that he was soon able to afford thanks to booming sales in Mülln, which was supposed to promote his creation as »Bosa«. However, the sign painter, perhaps thinking of Bosnia, added an »n«. Whatever the story, as Bosna (with the feminine definite article in German: »die«), Todoroff's speciality became an instant classic.

Over 60 years later, Salzburg's fast-food version still tastes best at the »Balkan Grill« or »1. Salzburger Bosna Grill«, as announced by a neon sign.

On good days, 800 servings pass across the counter, and the cult snack is offered in five variations. The base, however, is always two pieces of pork sausage fresh from the butcher, who has owned the stall for a long time, as well as curry powder.

Address In the passageway between Getreidegasse 33 and Universitatsplatz 2, A-5020 Salzburg | Opening times daily 11am–7pm, Sat 11am–6pm, Sun 2–7pm | Public transport Buses no. 1, 4, 8, 22, stop Herbert-von-Karajan Platz | Tip Don't be put off by the long queues; things move quickly inside the sausage stall. Sausage aficionados will find an even larger selection at the Grünmarkt on Universitätsplatz square.

23__ The Baptismal Font
A rite of passage from Mozart to Mohr

Entering the cathedral by its mighty doors, a left turn leads to the first lateral chapel, and in its centre you'll see a large bronze baptismal font. This is a place where the centuries in Salzburg start to dissolve into a haze. According to an inscription it was created in 1321 by a Master Heinrich (Henry), while the bronze lions supporting the font probably date back to 1160.

Reliefs representing Salzburg saints, bishops and abbots adorn the rim of the font. The cover, made only in 1959 by sculptor Toni Schneider-Manzell, shows twelve motifs from the Old and New Testament, all connected to baptism, water and resurrection. Among other things, they depict the Baptism of Christ and Noah's Ark, as well as Moses striking water from the rock.

The font has been used for liturgical purposes for hundreds of years. It stood previously in the Romanesque cathedral, which was torn down following a fire in 1598. When the new Baroque cathedral was inaugurated in 1628, the font took its place there. The baptismal records have come down to us from the 17th century onwards. Those who saw the light of day in the cathedral parish – corresponding more or less to today's Old Town – would have been received into the Christian congregation over this baptismal font. On 28 January 1756, for instance, city chaplain Lamprecht baptized a boy from Getreidegasse, who went on to world fame under the name Wolfgang Amadeus Mozart. »Joannes Chrysostomus Wolfgangus Theophilus« is what it says in the parish register.

On 11 December 1792, a certain Joseph Mohr was given the sacrament of baptism in the cathedral. His godfather was the executioner Wohlmuth, who did however get a stand-in for the moment when the boy was being held above the basin. Mohr was to be immortalised as the poet of the »Silent Night« hymn, which on Christmas Eve rings out through the cathedral. Today, the cathedral sees very few christenings, as hardly any children are born in the cathedral parish.

Address Domplatz 1a, A-5020 Salzburg, tel. +43 (0)662/80477950, www.salzburger-
dom.at | Opening times Jan, Feb and Nov Mon–Sat 8am–5pm, Sun 1–5pm; March,
April, Oct and Dec Mon–Sat 8am–6pm, Sun 1–6pm; May–Sept Mon–Sat 8am–7pm,
Sun 1–7pm | Public transport Buses no. 3, 5, 6, 7, 8, 20, 25, 28, 160, 170, stop Mozart-
steg/Rudolfskai | Tip The Late Roman choir crypt shelters the 'Vanitas' installation by
Christoph Boltanski, representing the transience and emptiness of the material world
in an interplay of light and shadow and a monotonous speaking clock.

24 __ The Birthplace of a poet: Georg Trakl

Caught between dream and reality

»In blue spring the soul falls silent.« Pure melancholy, this is characteristic of the life and work of Georg Trakl. This extract from »In
Darkness« is taken from a poetry plaque, of which there are seven
more in the city. As the co-founder of German Expressionism, Trakl
(1887–1914) ranks among the most important poets in the German
language. At his birthplace in the Old Town, an exhibition, a modern installation in white lettering and a bronze panel keep the mem-
ory of the great poet alive.

»I am always sad when I'm happy.« This is a typical Trakl quote
from the documentary shown at the start of any guided tour. Images,
autographs, precious original furniture, a bust and a sombre self-por-
trait sum up a life that came to an early end after only 27 years, torn
between dream-like visions and a reality that was becoming ever more
precarious.

Trakl was the fourth of seven children born to a bourgeois family with good prospects in life. He visited an elite school, yet didn't
finish it, he experimented with drugs – and there were rumours of a
relationship with his sister Grete, which were never proven. His po-
ems, clad in virtuoso imagery, show two faces: a fine sense of beauty
alongside the depths of despair. Trakl scholars believe the decay and
destruction in his work to be connected with Austria, Europe and
himself personally. The realities of the First World War and the con-
comitant disintegration of Europe caught up with him during his job
as paramedic in Galicia in Poland. He was unable to bear the sight
of people dying miserably in war. Following a suicide attempt, Trakl
was transferred to an institution in Cracow, where he died of a co-
caine overdose.

The moving guided tours through Trakl's birthplace retrace the
life of an exceedingly sensitive man and poet.

Address Waagplatz 1a, A-5020 Salzburg, tel. +43 (0)662/845346 | Opening times Daily guided tours, 2pm, by appointment only | Public transport Buses no. 3, 5, 6, 7, 8, 20, 25, 28, 160, 170, stop Mozartsteg/Rudolfskai | Tip Poetry plaques can be found on the »Trakl sites«: Waagplatz 1a, St Peters Cemetery, Monchsberg, Schwarzstrasse 25, railway bridge, Mirabellgarten, Linzer Gasse 5 and Hellbrunn castle park.

25__ The Botanical Gardens
Salzburg's flora in a nutshell

From the bogs of the Alpine foothills to the Hohe Tauern, where Europe's most frugal plants defy ice and snow, from the tropical jungle to the desert – this is the fantastic journey visitors to the Botanical Gardens of Salzburg University can undertake across no more than a hectare of space.

Not many know of the treasures, harboured and staged with a lot of effort by the Faculty of Natural Sciences in Freisaal, and even fewer know that all of this is accessible to the public as an urban recreational space.

The »Nawi« (from »Naturwissenschaften«) gardeners have grouped together habitats typical of our latitudes into ecological groups such as bogs, Alpine or dry grass. Here saxifrage and lichens cling to the fissures in the limestone, while a few yards on a rivulet babbles through a slice of raised bog, shimmering darkly. Divided by pebble paths, together the habitats exude the calm of a Zen garden. Benches and leafy corners invite visitors to take a rest. An integrated watercourse with idling fish and the odd artwork further enhance the horticultural wonder.

Look out for the special and exotic features on view: for instance a calendar with indicator plants for the various phenological seasons, an island of carnivorous plants demonstrating the various techniques for catching and digesting careless insects, as well as a vertical hothouse with tropical plants.

The apothecary garden presents 280 different medicinal and curative plants of the region, some of which have been used for centuries.

That arnica, lavender and the general harnessing of the healing powers of nature are en vogue, is also evidenced by the numbers of people taking part in the special guided tours offered by Salzburg pharmacists through this 300 square metre botanical treasure. By the way, you'll also learn to recognise – and avoid – toxic herbs.

Address Salzburg University, Botanischer Garten, Hellbrunnerstrasse 34, A-5020 Salzburg (Nonntal), tel. +43 (0)662/8044-5531 (for guided tours), www.uni-salzburg.at/orgbiol/botanischer.garten | Opening times May–Sept Tue–Sun 10am–6pm | Public transport Bus no. 22, stop Michael-Pacher-Strasse | Tip The predecessor of the Botanic Gardens was situated on the site of today's Furtwänglergarten in the Old Town. Today still you can see botanical specimen such as a Weymouth pine or a mighty gingko tree there.

26__The Cabbage Guard's Cottage

Where the hangman didn't live

The little house sitting on its own in a meadow below the mountain fortress is shrouded in a mysterious aura. Half hidden behind hedges, shrubs and trees, it avoids closer scrutiny from walkers and cyclists stopping at the Almgasse and Hans Sedlmayr Weg crossroads. Understandably, people soon started to weave a dark legend around this old building standing so deliberately remote from everything. Somebody living in an enchanted place like this, it was said, must have a job that might be necessary yet tainted with an indelible stigma. Like an executioner. And so it came about that the building is known to many Salzburgers as the »Henkerhausl«, or Hangman's Cottage, which, as always, sounds much more colourful in the Austrian dialect.

The truth, as it were, is much less exciting, and it becomes evident once you give closer attention to the detailed Salzburg panorama on Residenzplatz square, completed in 1829. Here, the little white-washed house is shown amongst fields. And that small clue leads us onto the right trail.

For hundreds of years, the building served as accommodation for the monastery employees charged with guarding the vegetable fields of St. Peter's Abbey. They would overlook the vegetable patches, which, it would seem, did attract unwanted attentions, from the slightly elevated Krautwächterhausl (Cabbage Guard's Cottage) or Flurwächterhausl. Cabbage, or »Kraut«, was once an important food item, particularly in the winter months when vitamin-rich food was hard to come by – and was indispensable at the monks' table. Whether any cabbage thief ever lost his head here is not known; the real hangman lived elsewhere. Today the cabbage fields are long gone, and the pasture is part of the Leopoldskroner Weiher (pond) nature reserve. The little house is let, and the dense belt of greenery shielding it from view during three seasons helps the inhabitants to protect their privacy.

Address Almgasse 7, A-5020 Salzburg (Riedenburg) | Public transport Bus no. 25, stop Seniorenheim Nonntal | Tip For an imposing view of the Krautwächterhausl, climb the fortress.

27__The Carillon Tower

Salzburg's acoustic icon in view

The carillon of the New Residence has been an acoustic icon of Salzburg for over 300 years, with its melodies ringing out three times a day. The guided tours, which have only been offered for a short while, bring out new and unusual aspects of this tonal work of art. High above the Residenzplatz square you can experience the tranquil carillon drum which brings out the sound from the 35 bells big and small.

Grotesque creatures, half human, half animal, with arms ending in snake's bodies, accompany visitors to the tower. The splendid staircase with stucco work by Master Elia Castello is the first surprise. The mechanism driving the carillon is the second – a complex, beautiful to watch system filling the two storeys below the belfry. In its centre, a brass drum measuring some 2.5 meters/1.5 feet across and featuring 7,964 holes is the hub of the melody.

When every pin is in place, the drum starts rolling and the mechanism begins. Wooden slats move, pulleys swing into action, rollers and articulated joining rods transfer the information to the hammer works, which starts up the bell choreography.

Observing this is a pleasure and fills one with admiration for the level of craftsmanship at the turn of the 18th century.

In 1695, Archbishop Johann Ernst Graf Thun had the 35 bells brought up from the bell founder Melchior de Haze in Antwerp. The driving force behind the development of the propulsion mechanism was Salzburg court watchmaker Jeremias Sauter, and in 1704 he was able to announce its completion. Today, an electric motor and a timer keep the technical wonder running. And after restoration works completed in 2011 it sounds fresh and cheery again. Some 40 musical pieces can be set on the large brass drum. If you can hear wild tinkling from the bell tower, they are in the process of being reset.

Address Neue Residenz, Residenzplatz, A-5020 Salzburg, tel. +43 (0)662/620808-700 | Opening times Performances daily 7am, 11am and 6pm, guided tours taking place between late March–late Oct Thu 5.30pm, Fri 10.30am | Public transport Buses no. 3, 5, 6, 7, 8, 20, 25, 28, 160, 170, stop Mozartsteg/Rudolfskai | Tip Don't miss the hand crank and allow time for the view of the Residenzbrunnen fountain from above. The white cube of the Museum of Modern Art on Mönchsberg is at eye level.

28__ The »Cat«

Where the Everyman caller has to give his best

The »Cat« – this is the name for a bastion of Hohensalzburg Castle, which pushes right down towards the city. Today, the former defensive position above St. Peter's Cemetery plays an important role in the »Jedermann« (Everyman) performance by Hugo von Hofmannsthal, which has been staged at the beginning of the Salzburg Festival in 1920 on the cathedral square, weather permitting. You see, probably the most important of the four so-called Jedermann callers is positioned on the »Cat«.

Its big acoustic moment comes about when the arrogant big spender Jedermann is celebrating a party. Death steps onto the stage in front of Salzburg Cathedral, and at that instant the four strong voices spring into action from three different locations. It's an impressive scene when the protagonist, so sure of himself just moments ago, looks around fearfully as he hears his name being called. He can sense that Death is upon him.

For his version of the Everyman, put on since 2002, director Christian Stuckl positioned two strong-voiced men in the cathedral arches, one on the tower of the Franciscan church and the fourth on the castle bastion. This last voice needs to be the strongest, as it has the longest distance to bridge – 70 to 100 metres/230 to nearly 330 feet as the crow flies. On the way down his call must not fade to a croak or die out. The caller sends his long, drawn out »Eeeeeverymaaaaaannnn« from the bastion across St. Peter's Cemetery to the Cathedral Square, reaching up to 120 decibels (as somebody once took the trouble to measure). The wave of sound breaks at the walls of the Alte Residenz before finally arriving at the audience and its intended destination.

From the very back rows of seats you might just about be able to spot the »Cat«, if he didn't quickly disappear into the shadows once again. Sometimes a casting is even held for this key acoustic role in the Salzburg Festival classic.

Address Near the mid-way station of the Festungsbahn light train; seen from the Cathedral Square and Residenzplatz Square, the »Cat« appears as a prow above St. Peter's Cemetery, A-5020 Salzburg | Opening times The bastion is not open to the public. | Tip To be in with a good chance of »Jedermann« tickets, place your order straight after the publication of the new Festival programme (autumn) (www.salzburgerfestspiele.at).

29___The Catacombs

Inspiration on the edge of St. Peter's Cemetery

Crosses rising like flowers out of the churchyard, enchanted tomb arcades and the natural backdrop of the Mönchsberg lend St. Peter's Cemetery an aura which inspired Austrian poet Georg Trakl to lugubrious musings at the turn of the 20th century. At the back, a sight that visitors might recognize from Greek mountain monasteries: seemingly without any foundation, a small church with a low belltower is growing out of the grey rock.

Above, windows can be made out in the rock-face. These belong to the so-called catacombs, which are part of the oldest and most mysterious section of the cemetery and probably have their origin in Late Antiquity.

In the access area, an ancient representation in wood of the Dance of Death serves as a memento mori to the futility of human endeavour. »'When things were bad to God we went / Death did end all our lament'« , it says on one image. This site owes its original name of »Eremitorium« to the hermits who once inhabited these caves. By following in the footsteps of the monks, visitors will find themselves plunged into a rock passage leading steeply uphill.

Two 12th-century chapels form the core of the catacombs, sparsely furnished with a few benches and an altar. The little light there is inside is hardly enough to bring out the remains of old frescos. Little wonder then, that this mystical place is shrouded in legends. »It was in the concealment of these rock caves that the first Christians of Iuvavum (Salzburg) celebrated the sacred secrets«, runs one inscription, for instance. Another makes the link between the chapels and Early Christian martyrs around Priest Maximus, but none of this is documented fact. It is also not clear whether the rock caves would once have served as burial sites – the name Catacombs only established itself in the 17th century. One thing is for certain though: there is no spot more beautiful from which to view St. Peter's Cemetery.

Address St Peter-Bezirk 1, A-5010 Salzburg, tel. +43 (0)662/8445760, www.stift-stpeter.at | **Opening times** May–Sept Tue–Sun 10.30am–5pm, Oct–April Wed–Sun 10.30am–3.30pm | **Public transport** Buses no. 3, 5, 6, 7, 8, 20, 25, 28, 160, 170, stop Mozartsteg/Rudolfskai | **Tip** A visit to the monastery compound of St. Peter's is best rounded off in the Peterskeller, the self-styled oldest hostelry in the area (since around 800).

30__The Cathedral Museum
A hint of former splendour

With a 71 metre / 232 feet dome, eleven altars and space for 10,000 people, Salzburg's Cathedral is an edifice that is difficult to comprehend in its dimensions and ornate interior. However, within the church is the »Dommuseum«, which breaks down the history of the cathedral and the oldest archbishopric in the German-speaking world into dimensions much easier to grasp.

The collection of the cathedral treasury comprises goldwork, paintings, tapestries and many more works of art. Particularly noteworthy amongst the treasures here are the famous Rupertus Cross from Bischofshofen, 1300 years old, the beautifully wrought golden, dove-shaped pyx holding the consecrated wafer from 13th century Limoges, and what is said to be St. Rupert's travelling flask.

The exhibits are displayed to their best advantage in the baroque ambience of the so-called oratories above the central nave's rows of chapels. The cathedral museum's exhibition rooms are connected by the organ loft. Take a moment here to enjoy the unique view of the chancel. From this perspective the splendid stucco work and the illustrated narrative cycle with motifs from the Passion of Christ make much more sense than from the ground floor of the cathedral.

However, all this is a mere shadow of the former splendour, as during the tribulations around 1800, when the archbishopric was secularised, the French, Bavarians and Habsburgs all helped themselves to the cathedral treasure. The Chamber of Art and Wonders, set up in the 17th century, suffered the same fate. What you can see today in the southern cathedral arches is a reconstruction in the baroque style, which still raises the curiosity of visitors. Precious amulets made from ibex horn to protect from the plague, ivory woodturning work, mountain quartz vases, emeralds from the Habach Valley, mounted animals and many more curious objects are on display here.

Address Domplatz 1a (Domvorhalle), A-5010 Salzburg, tel. +43 (0)662/80471870,
www.kirchen.net/dommuseum | Opening times Mid-May–late Oct Mon–Sat 10am–5pm,
Sun and public holidays, as well as in the Advent period 11am–6pm | Public transport
Buses no. 3, 5, 6, 7, 8, 20, 25, 28, 160, 170, stop Mozartsteg/Rudolfskai | Tip The
construction activity in the area of today's cathedral since the Roman settlement is
documented in the Domgrabungsmuseum (Cathedral Excavation Museum) on
Residenzplatz (cathedral arch) – well worth a visit.

31__The Chamois Colony
»… on trails that no chamois ever trod«

»… to explore strange new worlds, to seek out new life and new civil-
isations, to boldly go where no man has gone before« – the motto
from the science fiction series »Star Trek« comes to mind when considering the origins of the small wild chamois colony on the Kapuzinerberg mountain.

Cast your mind back to the year 1948, when legend told of a
chamois from the Untersberg – or maybe from the Kuhberg or the
Gaisberg, reports vary on this point – who in the dark of a foggy night
cantered through Salzburg to climb the Kapuzinerberg, 638 meters/
2093 feet high.

The adventurous wanderer liked what he saw and established
himself in his new territory. The Salzburgers couldn't fail to notice
the exotic new addition to the Kapuzinerberg fauna. A few years later, animal lovers decided that he needed a she-goat to keep him company. The two got close, and founded the Kapuzinerberg chamois
colony, whose descendants you can meet today on the local mountain,
with a bit of luck.

At the moment, the pack comprises seven or eight animals. The
size varies, depending on how many animals fall to their deaths or die
of natural causes. Occasionally the gene pool is extended from outside. The chamois are looked after and fed by a volunteer »ranger«,
who keeps a small cottage on the Kapuzinerberg.

The easiest place to encounter the horned creatures is the eastern
and northern side of the mountain, which also has the feeding station. These skilled climbers find steep rock walls and nooks and cran-
nies to retreat into here. The proximity to the city means they are no
longer as shy as their wilder mountain cousins. Once, when a film crew
visited to take footage of the only free-range chamois population in
a European city, some of them were happy enough to come trotting
out for the shoot.

Address Kapuzinerberg, A-5020 Salzburg | Public transport Bus stop Theatergasse or Makartplatz, 5 minutes on foot ascending Kapuzinerberg from the Franziskuspforte gate in Linzer Gasse | Tip In the Franziskischlossl (Opening times Wednesday to Sunday 11am to 5pm), a former fortification, hikers can take refreshments and enjoy magnificent views of the surroundings.

32__ The Christian Doppler Show

The physicist who inspired 14 Nobel Prize winners

If you stand at a level crossing, the whistle a train emits as it draws near is perceived as higher-pitched than when the train has rushed past and is gaining distance from you – The Doppler Effect is one of those physical principles that even back at school didn't take too much hard work to understand. It is named after Salzburg-born and bred Christian Doppler (1803–1853), whose thesis on frequency shift, when the distance changes between the source of the wave and the recipient of the wave, gained him worldwide fame, albeit long after his death. The enormous significance of the scientist's findings for day-to-day life is shown by the »Christian Doppler Schau« in the Haus der Natur (House of Nature), including interactive experiments: no child can resist the invitation to grab a ball and throw it as hard as they can against a wall; a few moments later the speed achieved is shown. Whether measuring speed by Doppler radar, preventing strokes with the Doppler sonography, monitoring airspace or observing the borders of the universe by measuring the frequency shift in the light spectrum, today more than ever, the Doppler Effect is being used in medicine, physics, technology and astronomy.

Fourteen Nobel Prize winners were inspired by Doppler – just one of the pieces of information you'll take away from this well-presented show. However, Doppler suffered the same fate as many other Austrian visionaries: his genius was not recognised, he had to deal with hostility and was only to find recognition in Prague. In 1853, the natural scientist died in Venice where he had hoped to cure a lung complaint. The exact spot of his grave in the cemetery of San Michele is no longer known – mirroring in a way another of Salzburg's geniuses little appreciated during their lifetime: Wolfgang Amadeus Mozart. Today, a clinic, a high school and a street in Salzburg, as well as a sweet, bear Doppler's name.

GEBURTSHAUS DES PHYSIKERS
CHRISTIAN DOPPLER
ENTDECKERS DES NACH IHM BENANNTEN
ASTROPHYSISCHEN PRINZIPS·
GEB·29·NOVEMBER 1803·GEST·17·MÄRZ 1853
Zu seinem hundertsten Geburtsfeste
die Gesellschaft für Salzburger Landeskunde

Adress Haus der Natur, 2nd floor, Museumsplatz 5, A-5020 Salzburg, tel. +43 (0)662/
842653, www.hausdernatur.at | **Opening times** daily 9am – 5pm | **Public transport**
Buses no. 1, 4, 7, 8, 20, 22, 24, 27, 28, stop Monchsbergaufzug | **Tip** A plaque at his
birthplace on Makartplatz 1 also commemorates the physicist.

33__The City Hall Tower

For whom the beer bell tolls

Since 2012, following a renovation campaign lasting several years, Salzburg's city hall has presented itself as an attractive mix of modern architecture and old building fabric.

The most exciting stories for visitors are to be found at its heart, the city hall tower, dating back to medieval times; for instance, the one about the beer bell to be found in the bell tower at the top. Weighing in at about 60 kilograms/nearly 10 stone, the bell was probably cast around 1450. Its ringing at 10pm instructed the pub owners to stop serving, clear out the punters and douse the open fires.

The lowest and most imposing of the three city hall bells is the fire bell, which would once have warned Salzburgers of conflagrations.

Purchased by the city in 1407, this multifunctional building once housed the tower keepers, who would proclaim the time, and their families. Nightwatchmen doing their rounds in front of the city hall would censor inappropriate behaviour with a spell in the »Narrenhausl«.

In those days, anyone out and about after curfew had to draw attention to themselves with a lantern or by calling out. The original municipal law stipulated »Nobody shall dawdle on the streets after the bell has rung, unless he is singing or going about with a light«.

All of this is shown during a guided tour, which also includes a view from the platform. But the biggest attraction has got to be the old tower clock with its clockwork, restored and brought back to life again after painstaking fine-tuning.

The mechanism presents itself as a miraculous working of cogs, pendulums, gleaming brass screws and weights attached by ropes. The electronic bell system also drives the beer bell, reactivated years ago.

However, today its ringing at 10pm seems to signal the start of the evening's entertainment rather than its end.

Address Rathausplatz/Getreidegasse, A-5020 Salzburg, www.stadt-salzburg.at | Opening times Not open to the public, guided tours only for groups of 15 or more people, tel. +43 (0)676/3385419 | Public transport Buses no. 3, 5, 6, 8, 20, 25, 28, 160, 170, 270, stop Rathaus | Tip The ground floor of the city hall has good shops, while the columned hall on the first floor is used by the Stadtgalerie to exhibit work by local artists.

34__ The Erentrudishof Farm
Strictly Catholic, strictly organic

The Erentrudishof in Morzg, a hard-to-pronounce district in the southern part of town, is a gourmet destination whose fame reaches well beyond the city of Salzburg. The noses of visitors entering the excellent organic farm shop are greeted by fragrant aromas. Over here is fresh fruit and veg piled up in baskets, over there a display case of ham, choice cuts of lamb raised in the Tauern mountains, poultry and cheese specialities – all organic produce from regional organic farmers and from the estate itself. The shelves are full of more delicacies of all kinds: savoury spreads, spices, pasta and pasta sauces, special oils and much more, all of controlled organic quality. The friendly vendor tells us that every Thursday you'll find fresh char and trout for sale.

All this is thanks to the Benedictine nuns of the Nonnberg convent, owners of the Erentrudishof in the south of Salzburg. By the time the first big organic wave reached Central Europe in the mid-1980s, the nuns had already been working successfully in organic farming for a decade. The catalyst was the first oil crisis in the 1970s, sparking a change of production mode to conform to the guidelines of organic agriculture. The necessary know-how was acquired in Switzerland from Hans Müller, an internationally renowned expert on agriculture and pioneer of organic farming.

These days, the Erentrudishof has long established itself as a model operation of organic agriculture. Since 2000, the estate is no longer managed by the nuns, but by a family of leaseholders dedicating themselves to pasture, grassland and dairy farming on some 78 hectares. Wheat, rye, oats, spelt and barley are grown, while some 30 cows provide high-quality raw milk which can be purchased round the clock from a dispensing machine. Bull fattening, raising young cattle and producing free-range eggs from about 400 hens complement the range of activities.

Address Morzger Straße 40, A-5020 Salzburg (Morzg), tel. +43 (0) 662/822858 |
Opening times daily 9am–6.30pm, Sat 9am–12 noon | Public transport Bus no. 25,
stop Kleingmain, around 5 minutes on foot | Tip Both Hellbrunn Castle and Hellbrunn
Zoo are near the Erentrudishof, and both are on the bus route no. 25.

35 __ The Festival Area Asphalt

»Golden carpet« for a select audience?

Is it just us or does the asphalt in the Festival zone have a different shimmer to it, just that little bit more dignified? The truth is, particularly at night and under festive lighting, the street surface yields a shine all its own.

This pavement is special. Various adjectives have been used to describe its colouring – golden, golden yellow, yellow, yellow-grey, cream-coloured, honey-coloured or simply beige – this variety alone is probably enough to illustrate the fact that the paving invites different interpretations.

When the special asphalt was first laid out, in the Mozart anniversary year of 2006 in front of the Great Festival Hall in Hofstallgasse, as the place to be seen for festival visitors, it created a major summer drama.

Some were cross that the carpet rolled out for the international festival set with their lined-up luxury vehicles was not just red but »golden«. Which is why there was a little schadenfreude going on when the »designer asphalt« or »luxury asphalt« lost its shine within a short time.

Unfortunately a faulty bonding agent had been applied, which soon covered the coat in unsightly skid marks, giving it a shabby look. To make matters worse it turned out this was not the only chemical damage. The urine of the fiacre (carriage) horses was starting to attack the top coat as well. Just three years later the asphalt had to be restored with a more resistant version of the »Splitt Mastix Coating«.

Since then the fuss has died down a bit, and Salzburg's climate, traffic and horses have made sure the new asphalt too has already swapped its original colour for a lighter version.

Address Hofstallgasse/Max-Reinhardt-Platz, A-5020 Salzburg | Public transport Buses no. 1, 4, 8, 22, stop Herbert-von-Karajan-Platz | Tip Max-Reinhardt-Platz square is framed by several artworks from the Salzburg Foundation, amongst them Erwin Wurm's cucumber sculptures.

36__ The Festival Open-Air Organ

Sleeping Beauty woken after 50 years

Organs that transport the sound outside are very rare around the globe. But the musical metropolis of Salzburg boasts not one but three of these rarities: the 500-year-old Salzburg Bull atop the Castle, the organ of the Mechanical Theatre in Hellbrunn, just half that age, and the open-air organ at the »House for Mozart« in the Festival area. The latter was in a Sleeping Beauty slumber for 50 years before being restored with much effort. Since 2012, during Festival times it has once again sent its deep sounds from the Toscanini Hof out into the city.

Covered in green rust, the organ pipes sticking to the wall of the stage tower erected by Clemens Holzmeister are an eye-catcher in the otherwise none too pretty Toscanini Hof. The organ has its origin in the early Festival history in the 1920s and would be sounded, for instance, when »Everyman« had to wander across from the Cathedral Square due to bad weather or during one of Max Reinhardt's legendary stagings of Goethe's »Faust I« in the Rock Riding School.

During reconstruction work in 1936, the instrument was granted a new lease of life when the third manual (i.e. keyboard) became the »open-air organ«. A further reconstruction of the festival site 27 years later led to the removal of the indoor organ, while the outdoor organ fell silent and descended into oblivion.

About half a century later somebody remembered the musical gem and realised during an inspection that it could be repaired. The restoration cost 300,000 euros: the dusty pipes were cleaned, those missing rebuilt to the original specifications, and a new mobile console manufactured, to breathe new life into the open-air organ. Since 2012 the organ is again part of the musical work of art that is Salzburg, ringing out for the opening of the Salzburg Festival or before the concerts on weekend mornings.

Address Toscanini-Hof, A-5020 Salzburg, tel. +43 (0)662 / 80450,
www.salzburgerfestspiele.at | Public transport Buses no. 1, 4, 8, 22, stop
Herbert-von-Karajan-Platz | Tip Resch & Lieblich in Toscanini-Hof serves
good home cooking at moderate prices and during festival time is often
used by stage workers – sometimes providing a good source of the latest gossip.

37__ The Festival Open-air Cinema

Opera and concert highlights for free

Today, Mozart's comic opera »Le nozze di Figaro«, tomorrow »La Boheme« by Giacomo Puccini with Salzburg's darling Anna Netrebko playing Mimi, and the day after tomorrow a high-class orchestral concert conducted by Claudio Abbado; what sounds like a concert wishlist for the coming Festival season, addressed to Salzburg's Santa Claus – and one that would be available, if at all, only at great cost – has become reality thanks to the modern technology used for the Festival nights on the Kapitelplatz square.

Every evening, for over a month, this »Festival for All« – sponsored by an international company and also known as the »Festival for the man on the street« – offers music lovers the opportunity to enjoy some of the top productions of past years in excellent sound and image quality. Add to that a luxury that no other festival is able to indulge in: showing highlights of the current season from the Great Festival Hall or the Rock Riding School, just a stone's throw away, with only a minor time delay.

The starring role is taken by an LED cinema screen, measuring ten by eight metres (33 by 26 feet) across, which can be used in daylight. This is complimented by a sound system that can be calibrated by the decibel to the acoustic conditions on the square. The advantages are obvious: you don't have to don evening wear on Kapitelplatz, and the ambience is more laid-back than inside the Festival zone. The culinary side of things is not neglected either. And to round things off, this musical experience is free of charge. The ambience can sometimes take on a certain kitschy touch towards the end of the evening when the last light of day dips the castle in a mellow pink and a starry canopy sparkles above the audience. The open-air cinema at least relieves the Festival organisers of one of their worries: not being able to offer enough tickets for all music lovers.

Address Kapitelplatz, A-5020 Salzburg | Opening times Late July–early Sept 8pm;
Fri–Sun 4pm opera films for children; for a list of events see www.siemens.at/
festspielnaechte | Public transport Buses no. 3, 5, 6, 7, 8, 20, 25, 28, 160, 170, stop
Mozartsteg/Rudolfskai | Tip The history of the Salzburg Festival is excellently
documented in the Salzburg Museum at nearby Mozartplatz 1.

38 The Flamingo Colony
Screeching and squawking by the zoo

Walkers and cyclists reckon they're in the wrong film when their wanderings through Salzburg lead them for the first time on to the Wolfgang Schaffler Weg in the Riedenburg part of town.

There is a screeching and squawking in the air that becomes louder with every step. And then a gap in a wall of elderflower bushes reveals a sight straight from »Out of Africa«: pale pink dots in front of a dark-green background, which at second glance turn out actually to be flamingoes. They are stalking around the shallow waters of a pond, throwing their necks far back, flapping their wings and making a clamour.

The birds populating one of the St. Peter ponds are not mass escapees from Hellbrunn Zoo (where sometimes animals, cheetah and lynx in particular, find ways to freedom), but part of a small private zoo that an animal lover and breeder set up on the rented lakes. There are at least 50, 60 or 70 animals here; overall there are said to be more than 100.

The flamingoes spend the winter in their refuge too. At the back of their stronghold, protected by a thick wall of vegetation, even though they are far from Africa the feathered friends enjoy the good life, doing what flamingoes like to do: some resting on one leg, others filtering out small creatures from the water with their beaks, others again showing off and enacting courtship displays.

The fenced-in area diagonally opposite also seems to belong to the ensemble of the private zoo.

First of all you have the grey geese defending their meadow with mighty honking sounds. Small cockerels strut about, while the shed next door is used by rare Swabian-Hallian domestic pigs as a shelter against the burning sun.

And the passers-by, who are enjoying these animal pleasures for the first time, see the exotic vista as an enriching experience.

Address Wolfgang-Schaffler-Weg (connection between Schwimmschulstrasse and Leopoldskroner Allee), A-5020 Salzburg (Riedenburg) | **Public transport** Bus no. 25, stop Seniorenheim (old people's home) Nonntal, then about 10 minutes on foot | **Tip** In contrast to their wild relatives, the flamingoes at Hellbrunn Zoo may be observed close up.

39 __ The Fotohof

A precise view of Salzburg and the rest of the world

The fact that an internationally renowned centre of excellence for photographic art can be found on the banks of the Salzach, sometimes gets a bit lost in the perception of Salzburg as »festival city«, »Mozart city« and »World Heritage city«.

The Fotohof was founded more than 30 years ago, and recently the gallery started presenting its manifold activities in the context of its brand new city home, Stadtwerk Lehen. Salzburg's figurehead for artistic photography presents an open and transparent image at its new address on the square named after Austrian photographer Inge Morath. The generous glass façade allows initial glimpses of the ground-floor rooms and raises curiosity about the works on display. About seven times a year, the Fotohof presents a new show from across the spectrum of contemporary photography. Renowned Austrian and international artists are represented alongside rising talents.

Admission is free, and that also applies to one of the best specialised libraries in the country. You'll find every important name in photography in the Fotohof's treasure trove of books: from the documentary masterpieces of the famous Magnum photographers' cooperative and works by Robert Mapplethorpe and Annie Leibovitz, to the landscape and architecture panoramas by Austrian Margherita Spiluttini. Many of the volumes were published by the associated publishing house.

What is particularly original is the chance to borrow fabulous photo art from the art library's stock. The basis is formed of artworks from the Fotohof's own programme of editions, together with those of numerous renowned artists over the years.

The »Artothek« comprises around 80 works that may be borrowed. Mirabell garden seen through the eyes of Magnum photographer Inge Morath – now wouldn't that look just perfect on our own wall.

Address Inge-Morath-Platz 1–3, A-5020 Salzburg (Lehen), tel. +43 (0)662/849296, www.fotohof.at | **Opening times** Tue–Fri 3–7pm, Sat 11am–3pm | **Public transport** Obus 2, 4, stop Ignaz-Harrer-Straße; S-Bahn S 2 and S 3, stop Mülln-Altstadt or Aiglhof | **Tip** Another pioneering cultural venue is the Stadtgalerie (City Gallery) on Inge Morath Platz 31.

40 __ The Franciscan Church

Charming stylistic mix from Romanesque to Rococo

Church lovers will have a field day in Salzburg. Visitors short on time might choose to forego the cathedral, whose dimensions and ornate furnishings can easily overwhelm, in favour of the Franciscan Church. The interior of this house of prayer, which from the 12th century to 1634 also served as municipal parish church, combines artworks from various eras. The Romanesque and Gothic basic structure, the splendid baroque altar and the rococo elements combine to form a harmonious overall impression.

Visitors entering the Franciscan church from the Sigmund Haffner Gasse will first cross the originally Romanesque nave, which has a sombre aspect and is supported by sturdy pillars. Next to it, the Gothic chancel opens up the view of the light-flooded main altar. Light and dark, chunky and filigree – these are the contrasts that lend this church its unique atmosphere.

Its most important treasure was once considered to be the late Gothic winged altar erected in the late 15th century by the genial South Tyrolean carver and sculptor Michael Pacher. We know that this altar would have been bigger than the famous Pacher Altar in St. Wolfgang.

However, 200 years later, in the baroque period, the South Tyrolean artist was considered antiquated, which is why the Franciscans commissioned a new construction from Johann Bernhard Fischer von Erlach, whose 1709/10 version integrated only the Gothic Madonna with her blue coat and profusion of locks. The rest of the altar was scattered to all corners of the globe. Fischer von Erlach's gold-laden execution has its charms too. A »child-like Madonna«, was how famous German humourist Erich Kästner described his impressions, with around her a »winged kindergarten«.

A memorial stone in the left side chapel commemorates Pacher, who died shortly before the completion of his masterpiece in Salzburg.

Zur Erinnerung
an den Maler und Bildschnitzer

MICHAEL PACHER

geb. um 1430 in Bruneck im Pustertal
gest. im Sommer 1498 in Salzburg
kurz vor Vollendung der Aufstellung
seines grössten Altarwerkes
damalige Stadtpfarrkirche
...anerkirche.

Address Franziskanergasse 5 / corner Sigmund-Haffner-Gasse, A-5020 Salzburg, tel. +43 (0)0662 / 843629, www.franziskanerkirche-salzburg.at | **Opening times** daily 6.30am – 7.30pm | **Public transport** Buses no. 3, 5, 6, 8, 20, 25, 28, 160, 170, 270, stop Rathaus (city hall) or Buses no. 1, 4, 8, 22, stop Herbert-von-Karajan-Platz | **Tip** Visitors with a little time on their hands may discover picture medallions, fine portals, marble reliefs and other gems in the narrow Sigmund Haffner Gasse.

41__The Gabriel Chapel

*Mausoleum adorned by thousands
of colourful tiles*

In the Sebastian Cemetery lies one of the most mysterious and beautiful of monuments: the Gabriel Chapel, containing the mortal remains of Wolf Dietrich of Raitenau (1559–1617). The round, yellow-tinged construction with its green dome forms the centre of the cemetery, which Salzburg's archbishop had laid out around 1600 in the style of an Italian Campo Santo.

A glimpse inside reveals a unique splendour: the walls are clad in thousands of blue, white, orange and green tiles, forming chequerboard patterns in ever new variations, while inside the dome the overhead tiles shine in bright blues and reds.

The rest of the mausoleum is a feast for the eyes too. Four niches containing the figures of the Evangelists are on display, and high-calibre stucco work and paintings enrich the interior.

However, it is the wall tiles that surprise people again and again, as there is nothing comparable in Central Europe. Some art historians compare this to Venice and the Iberian Peninsula, others believe that the models for the wall design of the Gabriel Chapel could be found in what today is Turkey.

Islamic tile art in Salzburg? It's an interesting thought. Where Wolf Dietrich did in fact take the inspiration from for his tomb is not known.

What is probable is that court architect Elia Castello and master potter Hans Khop followed the instructions of their master to the finest detail when they set to work in 1597.

A plaque that the Prince Archbishop had made with an inscription for posterity says on it that he, Wolf Dietrich himself, had »provided in every way« for the decoration of his tomb.

In 1617 he was carried to his grave in a pompous burial ceremony – against his express wishes.

Address Sebastiansfriedhof, Linzer Gasse 41, A-5020 Salzburg | Opening times Cemetery: daily Apr–Oct 9am–6.30pm, Nov–March 9am–4pm; guided tours including the chapel Tue and Fri 2pm from Linzer Gasse 22, Infopoint, no advance booking necessary; otherwise just take a good look inside through the grille | Public transport Buses no. 2, 4, 21, 22, stop Wolf-Dietrich-Strasse | Tip Take a stroll through Linzer Gasse, Salzburg's most important commercial street.

42__ The Gstattengasse

When the sky fell in on Salzburg

The bird population of Salzburg has barely started its spring chorus when unusual activities can be observed around the Mönchsberg. High above the Old Town with its buildings built onto the rock, people who appear to be mountaineers can be seen abseiling, swinging from one section of the wall to another, knocking the conglomerate rock with hammers and rods.

The men on their raised wooden hides, called »Schimmel« (white horses), belong to a profession that is pretty unique in the world: they are mountain cleaners. They clean the local mountains, removing loose rocks and roots, and repair the nets put up to catch falling rock debris. If larger chunks are threatening to come down, they will stop traffic at the foot of the wall.

Their weeks-long service at lofty heights serves as a reminder of the fact that Salzburgians can indeed be severely threatened by the rocky, forested ridge in the city. In the Gstattengasse this was proven true in dramatic fashion. Overnight from 15th to 16th July 1669, mighty chunks of rock broke loose from the Mönchsberg, burying the row of houses built on to the rock, including two small churches. When neighbours tried to come to the rescue of the people buried under the debris, the rock gave way once more, burying many of the helpers. At the time, the 220 dead claimed by the disaster found their last resting places at the hospital cemetery and the hospital church. Later it became clear that this part of the mountain had become unstable due to too many caverns, cellars and underground corridors.

A Salzburg brewer purchased the row of houses and ensured that they would be reconstructed in a consistent style. Today, a fairly uniform roof slope extends from the Gstattentor to the Klausentor. The Gstattengasse is not exactly a shining gem in the urban landscape, and to this day a number of citizens seem to avoid any immediate contact with the mountain, deeming it to be just that bit too creepy.

Address Gstattengasse, A-5020 Salzburg | Public transport Buses no. 1, 4, 7, 8, 20, 22, 24, 27, 28, stop Monchsbergaufzug; buses no. 7, 10, 20, 21, 27, 28, stop Barenwirt | Tip Memorial plaques on the Ursuline church and at St Sebastian's Cemetery serve as a reminder of the avalanche disaster.

43__The Hangar-7 Aircraft Museum

Veterans of the skies in new splendour

Salzburg's little airport offers a landmark that many larger airports can only dream of: a museum exhibiting former kings of the skies that have been saved from the scrapheap, restored and polished from nose to tail, returning them to their former glory. These gleaming chrome beauties enjoy a home befitting their status: a futuristic, UFO-like steel and glass construction, »Hangar-7«. The initiative is down to highly successful entrepreneur Dietrich Mateschitz, who made his money from energy drinks; historic aircraft are his hobby horse.

Taking pride of place amongst the air fleet – and ready for action – is the DC-6B. Built in 1958, this was once Yugoslavia's »Air Force One« and used to ferry head of state Tito, and later African potentates, around the globe. Brought back from retirement in Namibia, taken to pieces and restored over years, the silver bird today does service with the »Flying Bulls«. As does the Mitchell B-25J bomber, which had already spent its twilight years in an Arizona plane cemetery.

Under the glass canopy, more historical flight contraptions – decommissioned Alpha jets, micro jets, helicopters and aerobatic planes await their next mission.

Competition comes in the shape of Formula 1 racing cars and motorbikes from the Red-Bull stable. And those left cold by the smell of kerosene and petrol might enjoy the latest art exhibition or Hangar-7's exotic botanical programme with its Phoenix palms, tamarind trees and elephant's foot plants. All of which may be admired without paying a penny in admission. You can also, after a coffee break, do some celebrity spotting. There's a real possibility that the machine you see rolling out is transporting a Lindsey Vonn or a Sebastian Vettel to a PR event at Hangar-7…

Address Hangar-7 at Salzburg Airport, Wilhelm-Spazier-Strasse 7a, A-5020 Salzburg, tel. +43 (0)662/21970 | Opening times daily 9am–10pm | Public transport Obus 2, stop Karolingerstraße | Access A 1 exit Flughafen (airport), Hangar-7 is signposted | Tip The »Ikarus« gourmet meeting point in Hangar-7 hosts an ongoing succession of top chefs from all over the world – a reservation is a good idea!

44_ The Hellbrunner Allee
A thoroughfare, but not for everybody

Almost no other town or city in Austria is as cycle-friendly as Salzburg. In the shape of the Hellbrunner Allee, an entire boulevard has been put aside just for cyclists; well, to be precise, they do have to share the paved avenue with pedestrians and joggers.

This route leads straight as an arrow through the green belt in the south to Hellbrunn Castle, built for the revelry-obsessed Prince Archbishop Markus Sittikus between 1613 and 1619. For a good 200 years, its use was restricted to the dukes and their entourage.

Today, there is no doubt that the way is the destination. There is much to discover along the three-and-a-half kilometres/just over two miles of the avenue. Former palaces of the nobility are testimony to their desire to be physically close to the rulers. On one side you have Frohnburg Castle shining in bright Schönbrunn yellow, where Mozarteum students reside and play music, while a gallery owner has taken up residence in one little palace, a manufacturer of traditional costumes in another.

In summer, the branches of the maple and linden trees, horse chestnuts, beeches and oaks form a near-impenetrable leaf canopy. About a dozen of them still date back to the time of Markus Sittikus. The old trees have long since become an important habitat for small animals. The crippled giants are popular accommodation among cavity-nesting bird species, as revealed by the chirping and clamouring. Rare beetles and other insects have also found ideal habitats in the old and dead wood.

That today the followers of sustainable mobility have this to themselves is mainly to do with a shock experience of urban architecture. In the 1970s, the plan was to create a new district from scratch alongside the avenue. The storm of protest against the destruction of one of the city's last remaining open spaces was successful. The Hellbrunner Allee, including the Fürstenweg down to the Salzach River, has enjoyed protected status since 1986.

Address From Freisaal Castle to Hellbrunn Castle, A-5020 Salzburg | **Public transport** Obus 5, stop Hofhaymer Allee or Buslinie 25, stop Schloss Hellbrunn | **Tip** Hire your own trusty steed from Top Bike Salzburg (Staatsbrücke). Salzburg's Dommuseum boasts a famous painting (with a copy in Schloss Hellbrunn), showing Markus Sittikus next to »his« Salzburg: the Cathedral is not yet fully complete, and the Hellbrunner Allee is still new.

45 _ The Hohensalzburg Funicular Railway

A trusty beast of burden

A fortress on an exposed mountain or plateau offers few creature comforts. Difficult to heat, it creates all kinds of other problems as well. One of which is how to haul up here everything that the inhabitants, or defenders of the castle in case of a siege, might need. The best option is a trusty and undemanding beast of burden, and for over 500 years at Hohensalzburg Castle this has been provided by the funicular, or »Reisszug« in the original German. Today, probably the world's oldest goods funicular still in existence remains the lifeline of the fortress, which in 2012 alone received 997,000 visitors.

From the Nonnberg abbey, the line leads through several fortified gates into the castle yard. Seen from the valley, it resembles a zip holding together the mountain that bears the fortress. However, the German name Reisszug has nothing to do with that, being derived instead from the »Reise« (journey, trip) and the »Zug« (train), i.e. little railway wagons, which in the olden days would be pulled up on a hemp rope more than 300 metres/some 330 yards long, a trip which could last two hours. The big rope winch was operated either by a group of up to nine men or by several draught animals.

The funicular was set up towards the end of the 15th century, on the orders of Archbishop Leonhard von Keutschacht. Soon it became indispensable for transporting building materials, ammunition and food supplies up to the castle. And little has changed to this day. Switched to electrical operation 100 years ago and modernised several times since then, the funicular still lugs food and beverages up the mountain for the culinary concerns of the fortress and takes the rubbish back down into the valley. Unwieldy goods, such as the glass display cases installed during the redesign of the castle museum, also travel the 80 metres/over 260 feet to their new destination by funicular. Today, the trip takes about five minute.

Address The valley station lies at the Stift Nonnberg convent, A-5020 Salzburg | Opening times The funicular usually works in the mornings. | Public transport Buses no. 3, 5, 6, 7, 8, 20, 25, 28, 170, 270, stop Justizgebaude (court); 10 minutes on foot via Kajetanerplatz and Kaigasse | Tip The Castle Museum shows a documentary on the history of the funicular.

46__ The House of Literature

Select reading material in a time-honoured space –
and in front of it

Stefan Zweig, H. C. Artmann, Thomas Bernhard, Peter Handke and more big-name writers spent important creative years in Salzburg. In an attempt to pass on the torch, the Literaturhaus Salzburg offers authors a platform to present themselves and their work. The schedule of book launches, discussions and events is dense and high-calibre, with jazz also finding a home here.

By Mozart's time, there was already much going on at this place. Leopold Mozart wrote that a »type of casino«, balls, banquets and wedding parties were staged here. Today, the former inn enjoys protected status. Parts of the corridors and the entrance area are still laid out with slabs of Adnet Marble dating back to the time of its construction around 1600. The halls, with their magnificent early-baroque panelled ceilings, provide a unique ambience for readings. International big names too, amongst them Allen Ginsberg and Herta Müller, once climbed onto the podium to read from their work.

Budding authors find support with the institutions based at the Literaturhaus, in the form of creative-writing workshops and advice on their manuscripts. Not one but two literary magazines serve to promote new talents. The reference library collects everything that writers with a connection to Salzburg wrote and how they experienced the city. The mediatheque then offers the opportunity to listen to recorded readings or the legendary interviews with iconic writer Thomas Bernhard in a bad mood, some of them with both image and audio. In September the literary enthusiasts offer guided »liteRADtouren« (a pun on bikes and literature) through Georg Trakl's hometown.

Also an original idea is the »Book Station«, a converted phone booth available as an openly accessible exchange for used books. Those afflicted by a sudden desire to read in the middle of the night can find what they need here for free.

Address Eizenbergerhof, Strubergasse 23/H.-C.-Artmann-Platz, A-5020 Salzburg (Lehen),
tel. +43 (0)662/422411, www.literaturhaus-salzburg.at | **Opening times** Mon–Thu
9am–5pm, Fri 9am–12 noon, mediatheque with sound and image documents:
Thu 11am–2pm | **Public transport** Obus 7, stop Strubergasse, Obus 24, stop Wallnergasse,
Obus 2, stop Gaswerkgasse, Obus 4, stop Aiglhof, as well as S-Bahn S 2 and S 3, stop
Mülln-Altstadt or Aiglhof, 5 minutes on foot from each | **Tip** Why not combine a visit
to the Eizenbergerhof with a hike up Mönchsberg, which provided the heights of literary
inspiration to Peter Handke and many others.

47__The Knifemaker Kappeller

Sharp and stylish

Garlanded with awards, the Salzburg knife maker Richard Kappeller is living proof of the fact that honest craft can still be a lucrative affair. It was chance that made him choose his profession ten years ago when he wanted to buy a knife, couldn't find any that he liked and decided to make his own. He ended up enjoying it so much that, following his training at the woodwork college in Kuchl, he simply changed his main working material, switching to steel. Just a year later, in 2003, the experts of the international trade in Solingen selected the corn-on-the-cob knife, cast with synthetic resin by this surprise newcomer, to be their »Knife of the Year« in the »Innovation« category.

All Kappeller knives begin as a design on paper. For the rough parts of the work, such as the cutting of the metal and hardening of the steel, high-tech equipment is used. Everything else is classic craftsmanship. Every curve, edge and pattern is worked with file and sandpaper for as long as it takes to reach the perfect union of technology and design. Kappeller uses the most varied materials, some of them highly unusual. From prehistoric mammoth ivory, from a narwhale tooth, stone or wood, the knife maker creates a handle as aesthetically pleasing as it is technically perfect. Nearly every piece is unique, with the occasional small series being produced. For a first impression, take a look at the noble knives online, or test their qualities in person at Kappeller's show room in Gabelsbergerstrasse.

Even the workshop of a knife maker, where work has to be conducted calmly and with concentration, sometimes gives rise to anecdotes. One day a strange order was received: a father-to-be had decided that only an exclusive Kappeller knife was good enough to cut the cord for the birth of his son.

Address Gabelsbergerstraße 15 (showroom), A-5020 Salzburg, tel. +43 (0)699/11806866, www.messermacher.at | **Opening times** Reservation by phone required | **Public transport** Obus 2, stop Stelzhamerstrasse | **Tip** 500 metres/some 550 yds to the west, admire the unique 1950s-style coffeehouse design of Cafe Wernbacher (Franz-Josef-Strasse 5).

48_ The Leopoldskron Park

Max Reinhardt's personal playground

No other castle in Salzburg has had such a chequered history as the rococo jewel that is Leopoldskron. It was built (1736–1740) by Prince Archbishop Firmian, who had been responsible for a merciless expulsion of Protestants and hoped the building would give a new lustre to his image. Georg Zierer, who owned it from 1837 onwards, sold paintings from a valuable palace collection at knockdown prices. Another past owner of the place was King Ludwig I of Bavaria. Yet it took the brilliant theatre director and co-founder of the Salzburg Festival, Max Reinhardt, to restore Leopoldskron to its true splendour in 1918. It was also Reinhardt who fashioned the palace park according to his baroque vision.

The park hosts valuable sculptures – including Hercules wrestling with a lion – and many artfully designed sandstone vases, each weighing about 1.5 tons. When the Nazis requisitioned the palace in 1938, they carted several sculptures off to Berlin to use in theatre productions. They were brought back subsequently, only to be thrown into the park. It took a lot of money and effort to restore parts of the park and 55 sculptures that were threatening to sink into the moist bog soil of the area.

Max Reinhardt also erected a baroque garden theatre with light-reflecting pools, walls with climbing plants and an excavated orchestra space. However, the only piece to have been staged here is Shakespeare's »As You Like It«, and even that had to be stopped because of heavy rains. Reinhardt's tendency towards the exceptional also shone through in the flora and fauna of the park. There were orange and lemon trees, flamingoes and a cage with two monkeys who were given the names of Salzburg archbishops – Sittikus and Firmian.

Since 1947 the palace and park have been the private property of the US »Salzburg Global Seminar« educational institution and not accessible to the public. Yet here in Austria, there is always a little exception to be made…

Address Leopoldskronstrasse 56–58, A-5020 Salzburg, www.schloss-leopoldskron.com | **Opening times** Accessible only to castle visitors (tour guide Sabine Rath can organise tours: www.tourguide-salzburg.com) | **Public transport** Bus no. 22, stop Wartbergweg; bus no. 25, stop Seniorenheim (old people's home) Nonntal then 10 minutes on foot through Hans-Donnenberg-Park to the palace | **Tip** The open-air Leopoldskron swimming pool next door (Leopoldskronstrasse 50) is a cool place to while away a hot summer's day in Salzburg.

49__ The Lightning Measurement Station

If lightning strikes, it'll be at the Gaisberg

With its broadcast mast on top, the Gaisberg is not only an important orientation aid, but also an unusual observation station. Nowhere else in Austria does lightning strike more often than on the 1,287 metre/4,222-ft spur of the Osterhorn group of mountains and one of Salzburg's local peaks. Or, to put it more precisely, the 100 metre mast point of the transmitter registers between 50 and 60 hits a year.

Science has taken advantage of this phenomenon, adding a lightning measurement station to the forest of antennae and satellite dishes. Its main exterior elements are the lightning rods, just about visible with the naked eye at the top of the red-and-white mast.

What makes this observation station unique in the world is the sheer quality of the Gaisberg's lightning strikes. 99 per cent of them are »upward streamers«, starting at the tower and rising up into the thunder cloud. While the sensors installed on the mast point measure the physical parameters of the hit, a special camera documents the event with up to 1,000 images per second. The authority in charge here is the Austrian Lightning Detection & Information System (ALDIS), which exchanges the findings with international partners and businesses.

The measurements help to understand the phenomena arising during thunder and lightning, and specifically during a lightning strike. There's no shortage of practical use either: the findings from the measurement station serve both to optimise the Austrian-wide ALDIS lightning localisation system, and to improve protective measures for wind energy plants in exposed locations, where hits often follow the same pattern. And when dark clouds rise over the Gaisberg as you're hiking on its slopes? Don't waste time looking for a beech tree, the experts recommend. The safest place, with near-zero danger, is right under the mast, which serves as a lightning arrester.

Address Gaisberg, A-5020 Salzburg | Public transport Bus no. 151 from Mirabellplatz, stop Gaisbergspitze | Access Via Wolfgangsee-Strasse/B158 and the Gaisberg Landesstrasse/L158 to the car park at the summit plateau | Tip On less stormy days, the Gaisberg »Rundwanderweg« circular walking route offers an attractive way to see the city and its surroundings from the most varied perspectives.

50__ The m32 Panorama Café
Where art meets antlers

The most beautiful way to earn your breakfast in Salzburg leads across the Mönchsberg. It's just a question of shaking off the morning lethargy, taking your goal firmly into your sights from Mülln or the Old Town, getting moving and not stopping until you reach the m32 Panorama cafe.

Doors open at nine o'clock. At that time the m32, in the compound of the Museum of Modern Art, still operates as a café instead of a gourmet restaurant or meeting point for hipsters. While the Early Bird Special of your choice is being prepared, select the most beautiful spot on the terrace and watch how the panorama of the Old Town gains definition in the morning light.

For an even more laid-back start to the day, we'd recommend nabbing a space on the red leather benches at the back of the café, where you can read the newspapers in peace and quiet, browse the selection of art books or just soak up the atmosphere, accompanied by unobtrusive lounge music.

The pretty, original furnishings also lift the spirits. Every time you take a sip of your apple-carrot-ginger juice, the eye wanders to the hundreds of deer antlers hanging from the ceiling. The cheeky chain of horns was interlinked and made into a light installation by star architect Matteo Thun. The »Lusterweibchen« (lusty little women) installation crosses the room against a red background, accentuating the glass frontage and the light-coloured exposed concrete. More nature effects are provided by the vases with antlers and branches.

A mirror along the back wall ensures that no-one misses what is happening on the big panoramic screen just a few paces further on. And that of course is the main reason many visitors come here. Others are attracted by the artworks in the Museum of Modern Art. But before you view them, get into the mood first, preferably with another coffee.

Address Restaurant m32, Monchsberg 32, A-5020 Salzburg, tel. +43 (0)662/841000, www.m32.at | Opening times Tue–Sun 9am–1am, at Festival times Mon too | Public transport Monchsbergaufzug from bus stop Monchsbergaufzug | Tip Once night falls, an intense interplay of light and atmosphere is offered by the walk-in »Sky Space« installation by James Turrell, right next to the museum compound.

51__The Magic Flute Cottage
Modest site of Mozart inspiration

Even if the story isn't true, it is well concocted: when in 1791 Wolfgang Amadeus Mozart accepted a commission for a light opera in the tradition of the Old Viennese magical theatre, his librettist Emanuel Schikaneder is said to have placed him under virtual house arrest to guarantee the timely completion of the work. This happened in a garden cottage at Vienna's »Freihaustheater« (Theater auf der Wieden), which was managed by Schikaneder and where »The Magic Flute« eventually had its first night on 30 September 1791. Looking at the variety of probably his most famous opera, Mozart's creative powers don't seem to have been overly constrained by the restrictions placed on him.

Today, the former creative workshop of the maestro can be admired in the garden of the Mozarteum Foundation. Its uprooting to Salzburg is a consequence of the Mozart cult, which started in the second half of the 19th century. In 1873, its owner, Fürst Starhemberg, donated the modest wooden construction to the international Mozarteum Foundation. Rebuilt in Salzburg, nowhere really seemed ideal for it. From the gardens of the Mirabellgarten the cottage migrated onto the Kapuzinerberg. Time and vandals left their mark there, so following the Second World War the building returned to the valley to be restored.

Inside, the furnishings are spartan, with an old table and two chairs. In any case, far too small to serve as a venue for the roaring parties depicted in Milos Forman's cinematic classic »Amadeus« (1984).

A poster on the wall takes visitors back to the year 1791, when the world premiere was being publicized. Also on view are two images showing Papageno, Tamino, Pamina and other figures, as well as two information panels on the history of the little house.

Once the visitors have left, the building is locked up again, and the genius dreams on.

Address Schwarzstrasse 26, A-5020 Salzburg, tel. +43 (0)662/889400 | **Opening times** Usually only accessible as part of a concert, best chance Tue during the free »Lunchtime Organ« events at 12.30; find the dates at www.mozarteum.at | **Public transport** Buses no. 1, 3, 4, 5, 6, 21, 22, 25, 27, 160, 170, stops Makartplatz or Theatergasse | **Tip** Whilst of course often being chock-a-block with visitors, Mozart's birthplace in Getreidegasse 9 is definitely worth a visit.

52___ The Makartsteg
Hundreds of declarations of love

They exist in Rome and Paris, in Helsinki and in Berlin, in Graz and Innsbruck – and lately they've appeared in Salzburg too. We're talking about love locks, which document eternal young love on bridges in nearly every big city in Europe.

This urban trend displays itself along the Salzach, on Makartsteg, which has been given a new flair by the countless padlocks (and has probably also gained a few hundred kilos in metal weight). Appropriately enough, as painter Hans Makart, who gave his name to the bridge, had a lot of time for pathos and sensuality.

It took a long time for this trend to take off in Salzburg. In May 2011, an official census on the part of the magistrate counted exactly 42 locks on the most beautiful connection between the two halves of the city, which is pedestrianised too.

It was decided to put a stop to the metal declarations of undying love by Anita & Edi, John & Cristina and all the other couples. The bolt cutter set to work, prising off the love locks and disposing of them.

But all to no avail. Soon the first new »I love you« declarations sprouted on the meshed wire fence. The authorities realised that love cannot be denied – not to mention the bad PR for the city, which likes to promote itself as a romantic hotspot.

Now there are hundreds of locks lining the curved bridge. Most are of brass, some shining in the colours of love, and there are also a few old and rusty ones enriching the forest of lockets.

Are the bike locks meant to be an ironic statement perhaps? And the question remains, what happens to the keys?

It wouldn't be a surprise if there was a key cemetery just beneath the bridge.

And what if you want to conjure up your love and have to locate exactly the right lock?

Address Between Franz Josefs Kai quay (at the level of Ferdinand Hanusch Platz) and Elisabethkai quay, A-5020 Salzburg | Public transport Buses no. 1, 3, 4, 5, 6, 21, 22, 25, 27, 160, 170, stopn Makartplatz or Theatergasse, buses no. 1, 4, 5, 7, 8, 20, 21, 22, 27, 28, stop Ferdinand Hanusch Platz | Tip Only a few yards from Makartsteg (left-hand bank), consider boarding the »Amadeus Salzburg« to explore Salzburg from the water (April to October).

53 Manufacturer of Leather Garments

Traditional costume from top to toe

What connects Marlene Dietrich with Caroline of Monaco, Austrian actor Dietmar Schönherr with Pablo Picasso and Emperor Franz Joseph I with Louis Vuitton? The trail leads to a small shop on Salzburg's Residenzplatz square. Buckskin trousers and woollen socks, leather hats, loden jackets and accessories are the trade of the leather garment manufacturer, and specialist in »Trachten« traditional dress, Jahn-Markl. The shop, Salzburg's oldest tannery, has been family-owned since 1408. At Festival time the small shop, measuring just a few square metres, turns into an unofficial VIP meeting point on the banks of the Salzach. Things move apace here – a dress rehearsal in the »Goldener Hirsch« hotel beckons, and the hand-made Salzburger leather trousers are waiting to have patterns embroidered on them.

The traditional shop is one of the hotspots continually redefining the relationship between Salzburg folk and visitors and fashion in general, and its Alpine version, the »Tracht«, in particular. This dynamic can be studied at leisure through the performances of Marlene Dietrich in the 1930s. »I can't sing, so what I wear has to be a sensation«, as the charismatic diva once said. The tabloid press would speculate as to what she would wear on her visit to Salzburg – an elegant costume with mink maybe? So it was an enormous surprise when she turned up in a loden suit and a traditional costume with a fetching little hat in Café Bazar, at the Festival and on Lake Wolfgang. The images of the style icon were to give the traditional dress look a leg up on the international scene and also served to get Dietrich and Salzburg »hooked on trad dress from top to toe, on nothing else«. One of the places she shopped at was Jahn-Markl, as proven by a signature in the client registry. To this day, artists and Festival visitors help to popularise traditional dress – and in exchange pick up inspiration from its spiritual home in Salzburg.

Address Residenzplatz 3, A-5020 Salzburg, tel. +43 (0)662/842610, www.jahn-markl.at | Opening times daily 9.30am–6pm, Sat 9.30am–3pm | Public transport Buses no. 3, 5, 6, 7, 8, 20, 25, 28, 160, 170, stop Mozartsteg/Rudolfskai | Tip The Salzburger Heimatwerk, on Residenzplatz 9 diagonally opposite, stocks a large selection of old-style and ultra-modern traditional dress. Make sure to visit the Trachten display on the lower ground floor.

54_ The Map Gallery

One of the most beautiful reading rooms in the country

The squares, designed following Italian examples, the monumental cathedral and many more of the city's buildings testify to the ambitious plan of Wolf Dietrich of Raitenau to transform Salzburg into a »Rome of the North«.

Only a few Salzburgers are aware of the fact that at the turn of the 17th century the prince archbishop brought a pictorial touch of Rome to the banks of the Salzach, in the shape of an exquisite map gallery. In the 1980s, this gem of art history unique to the north of the Alps was rediscovered in the Toskana Tract of the Alte Residenz and painstakingly restored. Today the map gallery serves as the reading room of the university's law faculty.

It seems that Wolf Dietrich was inspired by the Vatican map gallery that he'd seen as a young man. For the Salzburg version he had a hall, 23 meters/75 feet long and just under seven meters/ 23 feet tall, adorned with large-scale maps. These show Italy, Germania, Gaul, Spain, Sicily, Hungary, The Turkish Empire and the British Isles in bright colours. Amongst the artful title cartouches, you can make out ships cresting the waves with billowing sails, flags and other details. The templates were taken from the famous world atlas »Theatrum Orbis Terrarum« that Abraham Ortelius published in 1570 in Amsterdam. Views of 22 cities in Europe and the Near East complement the series of maps. The »Eternal City« is particularly well represented with ancient buildings and monuments.

With its collection of images measuring 90 square metres/nearly 970 square feet, the map gallery must rank amongst the most beautiful reading rooms in the country, possibly in all of Europe.

The only question being whether the law students are able to muster sufficient concentration for their studies in this atmosphere. A quick glance is enough to send the mind off on a journey to faraway countries…

Address Law Faculty Library (Fakultätsbibliothek), Toskana-Trakt, Churfürststraße 1, A-5020 Salzburg | **Opening times** Daily 9am–8pm; less in summer; the Gallery is open to the public. The library asks visitors to respect library users. Guided tours are possible in exceptional cases and only with advance notice: www.uni-salzburg.at /landkarten | **Public transport** Buses no. 3, 5, 6, 8, 20, 25, 28, 160, 170, 270, stop Rathaus | **Tip** Some 100 years younger than the Landkartengalerie, the Tomaselli Café opposite allows visitors to get to know the entire range of Austrian coffee creations, from the Einspanner via the classic Melange to »Kaffee verkehrt« (like a small latte, with more milk than coffee).

55__ The Marble Staircase
A baroque way to say I Do

When conversation turns to the marble hall at Mirabell Castle, wedding enthusiasts start waxing lyrical: »the most beautiful wedding venue in Central Europe« being one of the less poetic descriptions.

To enter holy matrimony in an ambience of stucco and gold leaf, where the musical wunderkind Mozart played concerts, is sought-after well beyond the borders of Salzburg. No wonder that there isn't much time for individual ceremonies. All the more reason to take a closer look at an arguably even prettier way to say I Do – the marble staircase (also called Thunder Staircase) up to the Registry Office.

Erected in the 1720s, the staircase is a masterpiece by baroque master builder Lukas von Hildebrandt and sculptor Georg Raphael Donner. The niches set into the walls are adorned by mythological figures – one of which is even a little risqué, showing Paris, who is said to have triggered the Trojan Wars by stealing the beautiful Helena, a married (!) woman.

The lavishly decorated balustrade is made from marble, its most conspicuous elements being the expressive »putti«. The chubby little boys accompany the wedding party up the staircase. But... hello, what's that?

The first one actually dares to tap his head with his finger. Which in common parlance signifies doubting somebody's sound state of mind. So a rather interesting contribution to the start of a way that is supposed to end in matrimonial vows. Is that the message the sculptor intended to convey? In any case, do slap one of the little angels on the backside – this is supposed to bring good luck.

By the way, same sex couples can also formalise their happiness in the marble hall; Salzburg was among the first cities in Austria to make the most sought-after wedding venues available to gay couples too, for civil partnership ceremonies.

Address Mirabell Castle, Mirabellplatz 4, Westtrakt (western wing), A-5020 Salzburg |
Opening times Visiting the marble staircase: daily 8am–6pm, marble hall: Mon, Wed, Thu
8am–4pm, Tue, Fri 1–4pm, no visits during special events | Public transport Buses no. 1, 2,
4, 3, 5, 6, 21, 22, 25, 32, 120, 130, 131, 140, 141, 150, 152, 154, stop Mirabellplatz |
Tip The marble hall's ambience can also be enjoyed during a concert (for dates see
www.salzburger-schlosskonzerte.at) or as part of a guided tour of the city.

56_ The McDonald's Lion

In Getreidegasse old and new get along just fine

Any merchant trying to stand out in the hustle and bustle of Getreidegasse must, above all, be original. The city, you see, does not tolerate neon signs.

This means that since time immemorial, artful »advertising signs« have been mounted onto no less artful cast-iron wall brackets sticking far out into the lane.

These are the real attraction in Salzburg's number one shopping street, as they tell the story of a changing commercial landscape.

Their origin lies in guild signs that showed the illiterate which goods and services they could expect to find where.

One of the most interesting examples today adorns the façade of Getreidegasse no. 26 – the McDonald's Lion.

For 560 years, from 1414, beer was brewed and sold here. In 1639 the »Golden Lion« inn was given its magnificent sign with the brewery emblem and the king of the animals above.

Things stayed the same when the building changed hands and became the Modlhammer-Bräu, and if the historians are right, the first public film showing took place in the rooms of the traditional inn in 1897.

The brewery closed shop in 1974, and after various interim uses, the world of hamburgers and fries moved in.

And because it's not easy to let old traditions go – and also because it would be sad to get rid of a fine sign as if it were scrap metal –, a sensible solution was found for the lane-side presentation. The centre of the brewery guild sign was given the famous »M« of the American fast-food chain and has since done sterling service as a combination of traditional and modern store logo. Further proof that old and new can get along well is the shop sign of a Spanish fashion chain a few houses further on.

Address Getreidegasse 26, A-5020 Salzburg | Public transport Buses no. 1, 4, 5, 7, 8, 20, 21, 22, 27, 28, stop Ferdinand-Hanusch-Platz | Tip The vast majority of the advertising signs in Getreidegasse were manufactured by the Wieber locksmiths, Getreidegasse 28. In the courtyard and corridor, visitors can admire fine examples of their craftsmanship.

57 — The Mechanical Theatre

And another one to the head

The hammer rises up before coming down in a flash onto the head of the bull. The animal sinks to its knees, seemingly breathing its last, before suddenly recovering. The butcher swings his hammer once more and the whole show starts all over again. Of all the automatic water features at Hellbrunn Palace, the Mechanical Theatre leaves the biggest impression.

The repertoire is no less than the life of a small baroque town. Here you see brewers stirring a boiling vat, over there a well is being dug; two soldiers are parading up and down, a bear is swaying to the sounds of an orchestra, and a barber is shaving a client below the sign of his guild.

One flick of the switch and the whole dance, powered by a water wheel, starts up. Wire cables transmit the movements to the figures of linden wood, of which only 21 are immobile. The other 149 are all part of the clever and sophisticated choreography, thought up by the Hallein salt-mine worker Lorenz Rosenegger 260 years ago. Since a comprehensive restoration, completed in 2012, the Mechanical Theatre – preserved in its near-original state just like the rest of the castle – works like new.

The organ workings too, are once again tuned to perfection, and do their best to drown out the clattering and rattling. To the tune of a choral piece by J E Eberlin, the duet »Give me your hand, my life« by Mozart or the labourers' song »Without Respite, to Work« by D. F. Auber, the representatives of every profession, from barber to roofer, go to work.

The creator of the baroque, multi-tiered tableau packed plenty of social history into his theatre; the higher up the figures are placed, the less actual work they do. The nobleman does nothing but guide the tankard to his mouth, and the lady on the balcony is busy fanning herself. Binoculars are helpful if you want to study all the entertaining details.

Address Schloss Hellbrunn Castle, Furstenweg 37, A-5020 Salzburg, tel. +43 (0)662/8203720, www.hellbrunn.at | Opening times April, Oct, Nov daily 9am–4.30pm, May, June, Sept daily 9am–5.30pm, July and Aug daily 9am–9pm; for dates for special guided tours to explain the workings of the machines see the website | Public transport Bus no. 25 from the main train station, stop Furstenweg | Tip Those visiting the Hellbrunner Wasserspiele with children should definitely bring a change of clothes for them. Also worth seeing are the works of art and collections inside the palace.

58__The Mitte Power Plant
Concrete instead of Baroque

Salzburg's Old Town owes its World Heritage status to its baroque architectural gems. However, since 2002 the concrete chimney of the power plant, 70 metres/230 feet high, on the opposite bank of the River Salzach, has been providing an architectural counterpoint. At night the power station-cathedral shines in blue, red or saffron yellow, visible from afar, while its silhouette is mirrored on the surface of the water, creating manifold effects of colour and form. The modern aesthetics of a bold industrial building – and pretty close to the much-vaunted Old Town!

The project by Swiss architects Bétrix & Consolascio provoked passionate debate before it was even built. For some, the anthracite-hued colossus represents an »eyesore«, while others praise it as an example of »liberating modern architecture«. An independent jury, which declared the power plant the winner of the national award for architecture in 2002, opened the floodgates of opinionated local debate.

In the end, the governor at the time refused to put his signature to it, so there was no winner at all.

Perhaps wrongly, as a guided tour through the inside of the plant shows. The foyer on the ground floor of the chimney surprises with sunny yellow tones. Forms that extend out, long sight lines and a warm orange reduce the technical coolness. The machine hall appears like a huge room of sculptures, while the turbine blocks are arranged like over-sized items of furniture. Two strong hearts beat in the belly of the monolith: a steam and a gas turbine. Transporting the 170-ton gas turbine from the Baltic Sea coast to the Salzach required logistical feats of the highest order. The turbine was eventually manoeuvred into the building on so-called »elephant's feet«, turned and plugged in. All in all, the Heizkraftwerk Mitte heat plant provides about 27,000 households with heat and another 34,000 with electricity.

Address Elisabethkai 52, A-5020 Salzburg | **Opening times** For a guided tour (lasting approx. 1.5 hours) book two days in advance, tel. +43 (0)662/8884-8903 | **Public transport** Obus 1, 2, 3, 5, 6, stop Kongresshaus (10 minutes on foot), or on foot from Makartsteg along the Salzach am Elisabethkai (about 10 minutes) | **Tip** The roof terrace gives impressive views of the Old Town's landscape of church spires, plus the castle and Mönchsberg. Josef Friedrich Hummel Strasse 1/corner Elisabethkai was the birthplace of maestro Herbert von Karajan, as visitors glean from a commemorative plaque and a monument in the garden of the estate.

59__The Mirabell Palace

A very special gift of love

Meeting and falling for an attractive man of the cloth, bearing him 15 children and spending the rest of your life playing hide-and-seek – it might sound like a completely overblown version of the Australian »Thorn Birds« saga, but this is what happened in Salzburg at the turn of the 17th century. The protagonists of the story were Prince Archbishop Wolf Dietrich von Raitenau and Salome Alt, the daughter of a Salzburg merchant. It was only his absolute power that allowed Salzburg's spiritual and secular ruler to maintain this liaison. There are even some suggestions that he secretly married his lover, who was able to come to him via a secret door in his residence, or that he conducted a sham marriage with her.

His attempts to have the relationship legitimised by the highest authorities in Rome proved futile. But this didn't stop Wolf Dietrich from building a palace for his companion in 1606 and christening it »Altenau« in her honour. However, the couple were not to have a happy ending. Following the overthrow and imprisonment of the Prince Archbishop in 1612, Salome Alt von Altenau became a persona non grata, moving to Wels with her hoard of children. She was to survive her »master«, who died in 1617, by 46 years.

There are few reminders of Salome Alt's existence in Salzburg. Schloss Altenau was renamed »Mirabell« and its appearance has undergone a radical change since then, being turned into a magnificent baroque palace between 1710 and 1721. Following the city fire in 1818, the former love castle was reconstructed in the neoclassical style prevalent at the time.

Nor is there any monument to Salome Alt. In its absence, we must draw upon the realm of legends. One tells that she is supposed to have invented the famous Salzburg Nockerl gnocchi for her lover, another that it was Salome Alt herself who modelled for the bare-bosomed beauty represented on the Susanna Fountain in the Mirabell gardens.

Address Mirabellplatz, A-5020 Salzburg | Opening times Mirabellgarten daily approx.
6am to dusk | Public transport Buses no. 1, 2, 4, 3, 5, 6, 21, 22, 25, 32, 120, 130, 131, 140,
141, 150, 152, 154, stop Mirabellplatz | Tip According to art historians, the burial place in
Mulln's parish church restored a few years ago was intended for Salome Alt.

60__ The Monastery Bakery
Nowhere does the bread taste better

The area between Kapitelplatz and Festungsgasse is framed by snack stalls and souvenir stands. However, even in this touristy corner of the city there is one experience that must count amongst the most sensual in Salzburg. To find it, just allow yourself to follow your curiosity and trace a strange yet oddly familiar sound that has its origin behind an old cast-iron gate.

And once you are standing in front of the clacking mill wheel, the incomparable aroma from childhood will waft across your nose: the divine aroma of freshly baked bread!

A few steps further down, discover the small and seemingly archaic world of the St Peter's monastery bakery. For a good 700 years, the art of bread making has remained practically unchanged in the vaults of what is now the last remaining bakery in the Old Town. The fuss is all about the »St Peter's Bread«, a pure, sour-dough bread which stays fresh for up to a week.

Water, flour and salt are the key here, with the rye coming from the best producing regions in the country, in the Lower Austrian Waldviertel.

A sustainable economy is also important here: the green electricity comes from the mill wheel outside the door, powered by the water of the Almkanal, and the wood from the monastery's own forests. The salesroom doubles up as the bakehouse, allowing visitors to watch the bakers shunt the loaves, weighing up to two kilos each, to and fro until they're perfectly done. On an average baking day, between 200 and 300 kilos/440 and 660 pounds of the »St Peter's Bread« leaves the ovens, in addition to two types of savoury nibble popular with tourists looking for a little fortification. You won't find any dairy products, soft drinks or souvenirs here. You eat what you see. The bread from the wood-fired oven is still warm when it is wrapped in paper, so that you're tempted to sink your teeth into the loaf straight away.

Address Stiftsbackerei St Peter's monastery bakery, Kapitelplatz 8, A-5020 Salzburg, tel. +43 (0)662/847898 | **Opening times** Mon, Tue, Thu, Fr 7am–5pm, Sat 7am–1pm | **Public transport** Buses no. 3, 5, 6, 7, 8, 20, 25, 28, 160, 170, stop Mozartsteg/Rudolfskai | **Tip** Wines from the estates of the St Peter's monastery, as well as liqueurs, are amongst the specialities that you can purchase in the nearby monastery shop.

61 The Mönchsberg Car Park

Spaces in the bunker are highly prized

When summer rain appears and the thousands of holiday makers within a radius of 100 kilometres/60 miles of Salzburg decide to take a cultural and sightseeing trip into the city, complete gridlock is guaranteed. Access roads become clogged and the narrow streets don't allow buses to pass, or even cars for that matter. It is at this point that a parking space in the Mönchsberggarage car park near the Old Town really comes into its own. However, the hollow caverns driven into the rock are well worth a glance for historical reasons too.

Entering the so-called »Altstadtgarage« (Old Town Car Park) B via the Toscanini-Hof yard, for instance, a musty smell hits your nostrils from several paces. A roughly hewn tunnel leads to the parking deck, past illuminated display windows showcasing the products and services of Old Town establishments. Moss sprouts on the walls, and in places the rock glistens with moisture. Everything is a model of illumination and signposting, yet somehow a slightly oppressive feeling creeps over you.

There is a reason for this, as the car park has its origins in the Second World War, when shafts were driven deep into the Mönchsberg, Kapuzinerberg and Rainberg mountains to protect the population from air raids.

Some 30 years later, when individual transport was starting to flood the Old Town, people remembered the unused caverns in the Mönchsberg. Using heavy machinery, rock anchors and sprayed concrete, the caverns were extended and stabilised. The Old Town car park in the Mönchsberg was officially inaugurated in 1975. With vehicles increasing in size, there are now only 1300 spaces available instead of the original 1470. By 2015, two more four-storey caverns will be hollowed out of the Mönchsberg rock, creating 650 new parking spaces. And those too will be highly prized by Salzburg visitors.

Address Hildmannplatz, A-5020 Salzburg, Tel. +43 (0)662/809900 | Opening times Around the clock | Public transport Buses no. 1, 4, 8, 22, Haltestelle Herbert-von-Karajan-Platz | Tip In the shops and restaurants of the Old Town featuring an orange parking sticker, the parking tickets are punched to give customers a discount rate.

62 The Mönchsberg Elevator

An early prototype for the Big Apple

Whether you want to work on your fitness by conquering the Mönchsberg step by step or escape the hustle and bustle of the city as quickly as possible, the elevator bridging the 60 metres/197 feet onto the Salzburgers' most popular local mountain in just 30 seconds is a good proposition.

The history of this elevator goes back to the 1880s, when a real race began to explore the potential of the local mountains, which were becoming ever more important for tourism. The Gaisberg was the first to be given with a helping hand with its ascent in 1887 in the shape of a rack-and-pinion railway (which ceased being used in 1928). Then the Salzburg entrepreneur and private banker Karl Leitner came up with a plan to connect the Mönchsberg plateau with the city centre by an electric elevator. A building in Gstättengasse was purchased and converted into a valley station, a metal structure mounted to the exterior of the conglomerate rock and provided with two cabins (eight seating and four standing spaces each). The panoramic lift celebrated its virgin ascent in August 1890. The journey took two minutes up to where a restaurant and viewing tower awaited the day-trippers. Spurred on by the huge success of the panoramic elevator, the long-planned project of a funicular railway to Hohensalzburg Castle was finally realized in 1892.

At 60 metres/nearly 200 feet, the historic Mönchsberg elevator was the highest in Europe at the time. It is said that it even served as a model for panoramic lifts on skyscrapers in New York. Until 1948, the elevator gliding up and down the rock wall of the Mönchsberg was a recognisable part of the urban landscape. Following the conversion of the terrace restaurant to the Grand Café Winkler, it was moved to the interior of the mountain. Today, metal bolts still visible on the rock wall of the Mönchsberg serve as a reminder of the external elevator. The most recent modernisation was completed a few years ago, in conjunction with the building of the new Museum of Modern Art.

Address Mönchsberg Elevator, Gstättengasse 13, A-5020 Salzburg | Public transport Buses no. 1, 4, 7, 8, 20, 22, 24, stop Mönchsbergaufzug | Tip The artistically designed entrance is worth a glance before heading up.

63__Mozart – as seen by Lupertz

A confounding sight on the »Walk of Modern Art«

A muscular female torso with a head reminiscent of classic Mozart portraits. A face lent a highly idiosyncratic expression by chalk-white skin colour, red lips and a mole. With his 2005 artwork »Mozart – a Homage«, German sculptor Markus Lupertz provoked controversy in Salzburg. It didn't take long for an offended sensibility to pick up a paint pot and vandalize the three-metre/10-foot bronze figure for supposedly »denigrating a genius«. The waves of excitement have long since died down, but the figure of the »female« Mozart on the Ursulinenplatz square still brings a questioning look to the faces of many observers.

Lupertz' homage to Mozart is part of the »Walk of Modern Art«. Started in 2002 and completed in 2011, this project gives those interested in art the chance to discover Salzburg through the eyes of renowned contemporary artists. The initiative came from the private »Salzburg Foundation«. Some artworks are very visible in the urban landscape, such as the ensemble of chairs by the performance and video artist Marina Abramovic on the Staatsbrücke bridge, the man on a golden sphere by Stephan Balkenhol (»Sphaera«) on Kapitelplatz square, or the Anselm Kiefer Pavilion opposite the Festspielhaus Festival venue.

Others can be found in places where you wouldn't necessarily expect to meet art. One example is Mario Merz' installation »Ziffern im Wald« (Numbers in the Forest) on Mönchsberg. All artworks are easily accessible on foot and open to the public at all times. Together they also provide the World Heritage city of Salzburg with new facets – and sometimes they happen to polarise opinions too.

Speaking of which, the protests met by the erection of the first Mozart monument in 1842 show that the composer was always good for a bit of excitement. A pamphlet denounced the fact that the Michael's Fountain had to give way to the »monument to a drunkard«, in the words of the authors.

Address Ursulinenplatz, A-5020 Salzburg, www.salzburgfoundation.at | Public transport
Buses no. 1, 4, 7, 8, 20, 21, 22, 24, 27, 28, stop Mönchsbergaufzug | Tip Every first Saturday of
the month, a public guided tour (2pm, meeting point Anselm Kiefer Pavillon / Furtwangler-
garten) leads visitors through the »Walk of Modern Art«. Advance booking required:
tel. +43 (0)664 / 4968011.

64 The Mozart Family Grave
Who exactly is buried here remains a mystery

At St. Sebastian's Cemetery, a simple grave in a verdant courtyard, always adorned with flowers, attracts much attention. A famous Salzburg name in gilt lettering catches the eye: Mozart. Of course, it's not the famous composer resting in the so-called Mozart Family Grave; Wolfgang Amadeus died in 1791 in Vienna, and the exact spot of his grave in St. Marx Cemetery is no longer known. Instead, the inscription lists a few close relatives.

First of all, there's Constantia (Constanze) von Nissen, Mozart's widow, who survived her husband by 51 years. Then you have Mozart's niece Jeanette, daughter of »Nannerl«. Mozart's grandmother Euphrosina Pertl appears by name, as well as Leopold Mozart. The composer's father, however, found his last resting place in the cemetery's arcaded vaults.

So why is this family constellation interesting? Well, in the run-up to the 250th anniversary of Mozart's birth in 2006, remarkable scenes were played out around the family tomb. In order to finally solve the riddle surrounding the »Mozart Skull«, which has haunted musical history for over 100 years and is today kept in Salzburg, it was decided to open the grave. The aim was to gather DNA from the bones of Mozart's female relatives on his mother's side, to compare them with the DNA information yielded by the skull.

However, instead of being the big media coup of the Mozart year, the hugely expensive »cherchez la femme« operation turned out to be a flop. What the forensic scientists found in the grave amounted to a mixed assortment of bones. A newspaper, under the headline »Total Confusion in the Mozart Grave«, condensed the findings as follows: »In the Salzburg family grave nobody is related to anybody else, nor anyone with the former skull bearer«. Who exactly lies buried here remains as uncertain as the authenticity of the »Mozart Skull« that a gravedigger reputedly lifted from the supposed Mozart grave in 1801.

Constantia
von
NISSEN
Wittwe
MOZART
geborne v. Weber
geb. zu Freyburg
am 6ṭ Jänner 1763.
starb hier am 6ṭ
März 1842.

RECTE GEBOREN 5 JAN. 1762
ZELL IM WIESENTAL

JEANNETTE
BERCHTHOLD
VON
SONNENBURG
PFLEGERSTOCHTER
VON ST. GILGEN
✝ ST. GILGEN 22. MÄRZ 1789
↑ 1 SEPTEMBER 1805

LEOPOLD
MOZART
HOCHFÜRSTLICHER
VIZEKAPELLMEISTER
✝ AUGSBURG 14. NOV. 1719
↑ 28 MAI 1787

EUPHROSINA

Address St Sebastian Cemetery, Linzer Gasse 41, A-5020 Salzburg | Opening times
Daily April–Oct 9am–6.30pm, Nov–March 9am–4pm | Public transport Buses no. 2, 4,
21, 22, stop Wolf-Dietrich-Strasse | Tip The inscriptions of the tombs in the vault arcades
contain many clues as to the former social structures in Salzburg.

65__ The Mozart Sound and Film Collection

Listen to the Master: 24,000 times …

In the annals of song history, Danish bass Peder Schram (1819 – 1895) is not exactly inscribed as one of the big names. Yet Schram was to create musical history in 1889, when he was asked to give a demonstration of his skills on his 70th birthday, which also marked his farewell from the stage. What was so special about this was that in front of him stood a brand new Edison recorder. In Danish, and a cappella, Schram recited the »Catalogue Aria« from the Mozart opera »Don Giovanni«. Together with the fragment of another aria it found its way onto a wax cylinder, which today represents the oldest known sound recording of a work by Mozart.

Anyone can listen to this crackly piece of musical history on CD in the »Mozart Ton- und Filmsammlung« (as it is called in German), which leads an often overlooked life in the former family residence on Makartplatz square. This is nothing less than the biggest specialist sound and image archive on the Master's life and work in the world. And there is no charge to use the library, where music lovers can listen to live recordings of concerts and plenty of material not available commercially. Some works can be called up in more than 100 different interpretations. Little wonder then, that artists sometimes pop round »incognito«, to find out how a particular score was arranged earlier. There is no shortage of eccentricities either. The »Kleine Nachtmusik«, or Serenade no. 13, for dulcimer and accordion, as well as interpretations by Mongolian musicians have found their way into the archive.

You can also become an ear-witness to moments when the odd interpreter lost their way mid-performance. 24,000 audio titles as well as 3,000 video productions can be played on demand there and then. The first relevant (silent) movie listed in the catalogue bears the title »La Mort de Mozart« (1909).

Address Makartplatz 8, Halbstock, A-5020 Salzburg, tel. +43 (0)662 / 883454, www.mozarteum.at | Opening times Mon, Tue, Fri 9am – 1pm, Wed and Thu 1 – 5pm | Public transport Buses no. 1, 3, 4, 5, 6, 21, 22, 25, 27, 160, 170, stops Makartplatz and Theatergasse | Tip Schedule at least an hour for your visit. In summer, films with a Mozart connection are shown on the big screen.

66_ The Mülln Augustinian Brewery

The supreme art of brewing, today as 100 years ago

Salzburg boasts a brewing institution for which its Bavarian neighbours – and beer fans across the rest of Austria too, incidentally – envy the inhabitants of Mozart's town: the Augustiner Bräu Mülln. The first and most important reason is the fabulous unpasteurized March Beer, produced by the monastic brewery founded in 1621 by the order of the Augustinian Hermits and today run by Benedictines. In addition, there is the modest price of under six euros for a measure and a beautiful beer garden.

So far, so well-known. But it's interesting to take a look behind the façade of the brewery, which to this day uses traditional artisanal production techniques. Apart from the brand-new brewing vat, brewing here at the Augustiner Bräu takes place using equipment that was the latest in brewing 100 years ago. The wort is transferred from the brewery to the »coolship« as it always has been, before flowing onwards via sprinkler coolers. At these stations natural oxygen is allowed to work on the pre-product – giving the March beer its »hearty« flavour. Another thing you rarely see anymore is the fermentation in open vats, and nowhere else in Austria will you see the use of a cotton filter for the gentle filtering of the beer.

The guided tours also allow a glimpse into Austria's last working example of a »picherei«, a brewery where the wooden barrels, large and small, are still clad inside with tar pitch. This lends the Augustinian March beer another special note. The lion's share of the finished product is consumed at the brewery pub right next door, the short transport distance helps maintain the beer's quality. Hoisted up from the cellar to the taproom, the 50-litre barrels are immediately tapped. That this craft brewery tradition sits well with innovative thinking is evidenced by the erection of their own mini power station on a nearby offshoot of the Alp Canal, which provides the brewery with clean energy.

Address Lindhofstraße 7, A-5020 Salzburg, tel. +43 (0)662/431246, www.augustinerbier.at |
Public transport Buses no. 7, 10, 20, 21, 24, 27 (on weekdays there's a direct connection
from the station), 28, stop Landeskrankenhaus (regional hospital); S-Bahn S 2 and S 3,
stop Mulln-Altstadt | Opening times Braustübl: daily 3–11pm, Sat, Sun and public holidays
2.30–11pm; guided tours of the brewery with tastings for groups of at least 10: by previous
appointment daily, afternoons only | Tip Its opulent baroque interior makes the parish
church of Mülln, just next door, a must-see destination for all lovers of art history.

67__ The Mülln Climbing

Parcours Peak feelings for urbanites

Paradise starts right behind Mülln's parish church – this witticism holds true not only for the fans of fine beer culture in the Augustiner Braustübl next door, but also for die-hard climbing enthusiasts.

For them, »Kogel«, »Buckel« (Hump), »Eineck« (One Corner), »Einriss« (Fissure) and eight more routes leading through the conglomerate rock of the Müllner Schanze, provide a diversion from day-to-day urban life, which doesn't exactly offer a lot of climbing opportunities.

Over the past few years, the number of climbing walls has mushroomed. However, climbing routes in the heart of the city as well as in the heart of nature, which are free into the bargain, are still the exception.

The walls of the former entrenchment, part of the Mönchsberg fortification ring, rise up 12 to 15 metres/approx. 40 to 50 feet into the sky. Plenty high enough to practise a good few grips according to Salzburg's climbing fraternity, that, with public support, adapted the unused rock for their purposes.

There are twelve marked routes in all – from simple via medium to very demanding (6+). As pieces might come off the porous conglomerate rock, climbers have to wear a helmet. Beginners and children can train coordination and dexterity at the foot of the wall. Boulders weighing several tons that were specially carted here from a quarry in Golling, are a good place to experience climbing without ropes or pitons. Climbing to »jumping-off height« is a good start to a sport that is increasing in popularity. Newbie rock climbers can also practise training grips and positions at a simple wooden wall called »Climb Master«, while balance can be perfected on slacklines. Some of the child-friendly climbing stations with imaginative names, such as »Pandora's Box«, demand a good measure of coordination skills from adults too.

Address Climbing parcours Müllner Schanze, behind the church of Mülln (climb the steps), A-5020 Salzburg | Opening times All year round | Public transport Buses no. 7, 10, 20, 21, 27, 28, stop Bärenwirt, then up the stairs | Tip At Mönchsberg (Richterhohe) too, you can watch climbers training – or partake yourself.

68__ The Münchnerhof

The famous »Münchner Kindl« still frequent this place

From the outside, this office building in Dreifaltigkeitsgasse reveals little of its glorious past. However, once you've stepped through the revolving doors of the Münchnerhof, a whiff of Grand Hotel wafts through the foyer. Wooden panelling, an enormous chandelier and tasteful decoration are testimony to an era when liveried pages still lugged wardrobe trunks around and parlour maids with lace caps hunted for dust. The real eye-catcher here is the dark oak staircase winding its way to the fourth floor, while hovering above is a domed roof light.

In the late 1920s, the Hotel Münchnerhof was one of the finest places in town and popular with German visitors to the Festival, which was still in its infancy. With the help of an electric lift, an air-circulating fan and other novelties, the Hofinger family who ran this establishment did their bit to improve standards of comfort in the Mozart city.

Some rooms were equipped with soundproof doors, each one had running hot and cold water as well as a phone, and guests would summon room service using a light signal.

After a bomb in 1944 left parts of the house in ruins and the US occupying forces had taken up residence here for a few years, the Münchnerhof wasn't really able to reconnect with the glory days. Converted into offices in 1960, the building also shelters a few flats. The good name and the furnishings from the interwar period are a reminder of its golden era, as are the conspicuous sculptures that greet you in the foyer. These are all »Münchner Kindl« – children of Munich.

If a hotel calls itself Münchnerhof, so thought the hotelier Hofinger, it should boast a few Munich icons too.

The one mounted on the outer façades was made from Untersberg marble, while the staircase Kindl were made in the workshops of local carvers.

144

Address Dreifaltigkeitsgasse 3, A-5020 Salzburg | Public transport Buses no. 1, 3, 4, 5, 6, 21, 22, 25, 27, 160, 170, Haltestellen Theatergasse or Makartplatz | Tip As the Münchnerhof is an office building today, visitors are kindly requested to keep their sightseeing discreet. The house opposite boasts a sgraffito freeze by Karl Reisenbichler that is worth a closer look – its subject: Life as a Card Game.

69 Neue Mitte Lehen

A monument to Salzburg's footballing overachievers

In the past, Austrian football clubs were rarely able to hold their own against the top teams from Germany, Italy or England. Yet in the 1990s Austria Salzburg managed exactly that.

In the 1993/4 season, the »Violet Ones«, with their home turf at the Lehen Stadium, fought their way into the UEFA Cup final, where they lost to Inter Milan.

The following season they even qualified for the group phase of the Champions League, before only just being eliminated by the future finalists Ajax Amsterdam and AC Milan – an unforgettable era for the fans of a professional team from the Alpine country.

In 2006 the stadium, which had become too small, was pulled down. Its successor – Neue Mitte Lehen – brought a long-overdue revaluation for this none-too-attractive part of town. Where the eastern stands had been, flats and an events venue rose up, while the western side was given over to the new municipal library, which was awarded the European Steel Construction Award 2009.

The pitch in between was preserved as a green space, intended to keep alive the memories of the old Lehen Stadium so passionately beloved by its supporters.

Today, children play where once the favourites of Salzburg's football fans would take to the pitch and where world-class footballers such as Lothar Matthäus, Edgar Davids or Luis Figo graced the turf during European cup fixtures.

The municipal library is a striking piece of architecture worth visiting both for its outside and interior. The tower, with a panoramic bar, is a new symbol for this part of town, but did meet with some criticism. Inside, around 180,000 items are housed across a surface area of 5,000 square metres. Some 15 per cent of the city's residents are regular visitors to their library – securing it the top spot in Austria.

Address Schumacherstrasse 14, A-5020 Salzburg (Lehen) | Public transport Obus no. 1, 4, stop Esshaverstrasse, Obus 2, stop Roseggerstrasse, Obus no. 7, stop Schule Lehen (school), Obus no. 10, stop Neue Mitte Lehen | Tip There is a weekly market every Friday morning on the market square under the gigantic projecting roof of the new municipal library.

70__ The Niederleghof
Both storehouse and obstacle to traffic

When Salzburg's tour guides funnel groups of tourists at one-minute intervals through the Getreidegasse, it's difficult to get anywhere in a hurry. You can always duck into one of the side passages opening up on either side, and head for your destination via the streets running parallel to the Getreidegasse. But beware, the passageways also have the potential to slow you down. A courtyard arcades adorned with flowers over here, a friendly cafe over there, and occasionally the eye is caught by an inscription that might arouse your curiosity. Such as the one above an archway in the courtyard of Getreidegasse 20, announcing a Niederleghof.

A plaque opposite sheds some light on the origin of this curious name: in the Niederleghof or Niederleghaus, as it was once called, which translates as 'lying-down house', from 1500 onwards merchants from out of town had to have their goods weighed and stored before being allowed to sell them in the town centre. The town would run the operation and be paid by the merchants for this service. While the repository initially included just iron and steel goods, the store room was later extended to cereals and wine, again allowed to be sold only here. The compound also included a mill, which was powered by the water of the alpine canal.

While the Niederleghof brought in revenue, it also brought plenty of traffic problems. The limited space already required complex manoeuvres from pedestrians, coaches, horse riders and occasionally cattle, now the loading and unloading of wagons clogged the lane to the point that an irate archbishop of Salzburg wrote to the authorities to demand the location be changed. All his protestations were in vain though.

And what do we learn from this? The Getreidegasse requires us to shift down a gear at all times and accept that detours are more likely to lead you to your destination – and possibly to a sight in its own right.

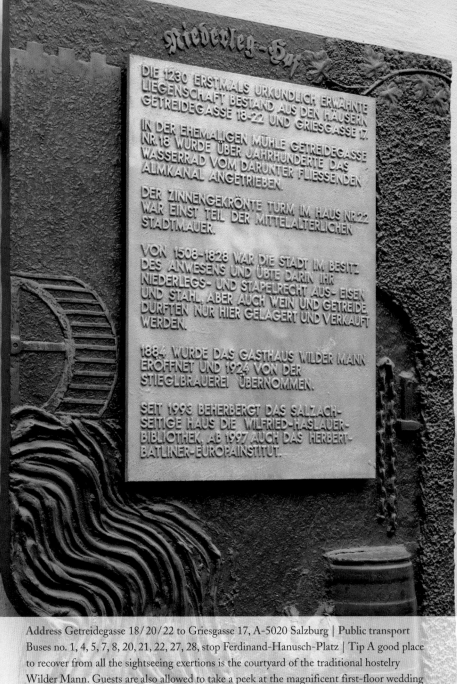

Niederleg-Hof

DIE 1230 ERSTMALS URKUNDLICH ERWÄHNTE LIEGENSCHAFT BESTAND AUS DEN HÄUSERN GETREIDEGASSE 18-22 UND GRIESGASSE 17.

IN DER EHEMALIGEN MÜHLE GETREIDEGASSE NR. 18 WURDE ÜBER JAHRHUNDERTE DAS WASSERRAD VOM DARUNTER FLIESSENDEN ALMKANAL ANGETRIEBEN.

DER ZINNENGEKRÖNTE TURM IM HAUS NR. 22 WAR EINST TEIL DER MITTELALTERLICHEN STADTMAUER.

VON 1508-1828 WAR DIE STADT IM BESITZ DES ANWESENS UND ÜBTE DARIN IHR NIEDERLEGS- UND STAPELRECHT AUS- EISEN UND STAHL, ABER AUCH WEIN UND GETREIDE DURFTEN NUR HIER GELAGERT UND VERKAUFT WERDEN.

1884 WURDE DAS GASTHAUS WILDER MANN ERÖFFNET UND 1924 VON DER STIEGLBRAUEREI ÜBERNOMMEN.

SEIT 1993 BEHERBERGT DAS SALZACH- SEITIGE HAUS DIE WILFRIED-HASLAUER- BIBLIOTHEK, AB 1997 AUCH DAS HERBERT- BATLINER-EUROPAINSTITUT.

Address Getreidegasse 18/20/22 to Griesgasse 17, A-5020 Salzburg | Public transport Buses no. 1, 4, 5, 7, 8, 20, 21, 22, 27, 28, stop Ferdinand-Hanusch-Platz | Tip A good place to recover from all the sightseeing exertions is the courtyard of the traditional hostelry Wilder Mann. Guests are also allowed to take a peek at the magnificent first-floor wedding chamber.

71 __ The Nonnberg Abbey

1300 years of solitude

Leave the worldly rush behind, all ye who enter! This could be the motto of Stift Nonnberg, if the oldest convent in the German-speaking area were interested in any contact with the outside world. Which they're clearly not.

For an almost unimaginable 1,300 years, nuns have been living here on the southeasterly spur of the castle mound, following the rules of Saint Benedict of Nursia.

Every step on the »Hoher Weg« in the direction of the nunnery seems to take you further back into history. Nonnberg's Benedictines, the two dozen of them still remaining, live in strict enclosure. Alongside the picturesque churchyard with its marble tomb slabs, faded epitaphs and cast-iron crosses, only the convent gate and the abbey church are open to visitors. The sounds of the city are very faint here. Once you step through the richly adorned gate of the late-Gothic basilica and close the wooden door behind you, the convent turns into a refuge of silence.

Inside, there is semi-darkness, the nuns having perfected the hermetic sealing of their world against visitors. The gold-shimmering winged altar or the late Romanesque frescoes of saints, created around 1150, are only revealed to those popping a 50-cent coin to purchase illumination time for the most valuable art treasures of the convent.

The crypt is also worth a visit with its free-standing pillars and ribbed vault.

The illusion of time travel becomes complete when suddenly a faint singing surges from behind the balcony of frosted glass shielding the nun's choir.

Chorals, which reveal by virtue of their rhythm and repetition a calming, near-hypnotic character, allow visitors to share for a few minutes the remote otherworldliness of this place in the shadow of Hohensalzburg Castle.

Address Nonnberggasse 2, A-5020 Salzburg, tel. +43 (0)662/841607 | Opening times Daily from 7am to dusk (summer to 7pm) | Public transport Buses no. 3, 5, 6, 7, 8, 20, 25, 28, 170, 270, stop Justizgebaude (judiciary building), 10 minutes on foot via Kajetanerplatz and Kaigasse | Tip The key for the Johanniskapelle chapel with its late Gothic altar from the Veit Stoss school is available from the convent gate.

72__ The Old Town Bollards
Steel nightmare for parking cowboys

For many a driver, these represent Evil in steel: the bollards that have been protecting – let's phrase it as neutrally as possible – the Old Town from unauthorized vehicles. The municipal authorities decided to introduce access barriers in order to free the World Heritage zone from the plague of the parking cowboys occupying every free square yard with their vehicles.

Of course, this wasn't exactly conducive to Salzburg's attractiveness as a tourism destination, ran counter to the concept of a pedestrian zone, and attracted the ire of a good number of Old Town residents too.

The introduction stage triggered strong emotions with some car drivers having to say goodbye to their customary parking rights acquired over the years, in front of the Cafe Tomaselli for instance, or at St. Peter's Abbey. These days, nearly 40 partly retractable bollards protect the Old Town at 16 points on both sides of the Salzach like a bulwark, rising up at 11am, the end of the general loading period. Those lucky enough to be provided with a remote control to sink the bollards were mainly Old Town residents, but also taxi drivers and emergency services. Traffic lights, signposts and warning signals make it clear to visitors and tourists that their cars are not welcome beyond the silver high-tech cylinders.

A census by the magistrate showed that the measure stops some 1000 unauthorised entries daily, which is equivalent to about a third less traffic. In the early days a good number of those who wanted to slip through behind an authorised driver were rudely hoicked up by a rising bollard and had to face a very expensive repair job on their car.

Even one of the famous fiacre horse-drawn carriages got caught once, as well as a pedestrian, who ended up injured. Since then spirits have calmed down, and the bollard's technology has also overcome its teething problems.

Address At 16 points around the Old Town (to the right and left of the Salzach River), e.g. Franziskanergasse, Getreidegasse, Mozartplatz | **Tip** Those who simply must enter the Old Town on four wheels can still do so by taxi – Salzburg's taxi drivers do have authorisation to enter.

73__The Parsch Parish Church
A crucifix hovering in the air

Remarkably few Salzburgers know this church, even though it is an important example of Austrian post-war architecture. Entering through the main doorway, the altar immediately catches the eye. The crucifix hovers in thin air, bathed in the rich light streaming in through the glass roof at the back.

The first modern church in Austria to be built from scratch after World War Two stands in the grounds of one of the oldest farm estates in the Salzburg area. This was the site of the Weichselbaumerhof, founded in 998, the only reminders of which now are the slim granite pillars in the seating area.

After the war, the property, expropriated by the Nazi regime in 1938, was given back to the St. Peter's Monastery and purchased a little later by the congregation of the »Missionaries of the Precious Blood«.

The church was erected between 1954 and 1956, based on plans by Wilhelm Holzbauer, Friedrich Kurrent and Johannes Spalt, who would go on to become star architects.

Other renowned visual artists were to leave their trace in the parish church as well. The relief panel above the main entrance was created by Fritz Wotruba, one of Austria's most important 20th-century sculptors.

The drawing »Fall of Man and Baptism of Christ« was engraved into the still-fresh concrete by Richard Kurt Fischer following designs by Oskar Kokoschka, one of the leading trailblazers of Expressionism, while Josef Mikl, who was also artistically involved in Hiroshima's Peace Church, designed the windows.

To local observers, the building's discrepancy between modern architecture and a subjective concept of art created space for fine irony. In typically Austrian fashion, they lovingly compared the glass roof of the belfry and the slanted roof above to a valley station, baptizing this striking detail of the church »God's cable-car station«.

Address Geissmayerstrasse 6, A-5020 Salzburg (Parsch), www.pfarreparsch.at | Public transport Obus no. 6, stop Fadingerstrasse | Tip Parsch is a neighbourhood with a high density of villas. A stroll from Fadingerstrasse in the direction of Kreuzbergpromenade reveals imposing examples.

74__The Patisserie Fürst
Made according to the »sweet« purity law

It's no use – ignoring the Mozartkugel is not an option in Salzburg. And the »Mother of all Mozartkugeln«, the chocolate created by pastry chef Paul Fürst in 1890, really does merit closer inspection. Not least as only this one may carry the name »Original Salzburg Mozartkugel«.

The recipe and the production method invented by Fürst, the master of all things sweet, have stayed unchanged to this day. The light-green marzipan core, shaped into a ball, plus a little pistachio, are given a coat of nougat, skewered onto a little wooden stick and finally dunked into dark chocolate. The sphere is allowed to rest on a board until the coat has hardened. Once the stick has been removed, the hole is closed up with chocolate – and hey presto! Every year, nearly two million »Original Salzburg Mozartkugeln« are made using this manual procedure.

In contrast to the discount merchants, this traditional Salzburg patisserie uses only raw materials of the highest quality, including chocolate from Caribbean plantations.

You won't find any artificial preservatives or flavourings here, which also means that the original doesn't keep as long as the industrial, mass-produced version. This is why Fürst only sells them in its four Salzburg branches – which manage to avoid Mozart kitsch completely, thank goodness.

However, the »Mother of all Mozartkugeln«, created around the centenary of the death of the great composer Wolfgang Amadeus Mozart, is not the only reason to pay a visit to the original and first Café-Konditorei Fürst on Alter Markt.

Here, you can also discover the Bach Cube, the Paris-Lodron Truffle, the Doppler-confectionery, the Salzburg Schilling and other house specialities. And with a little luck you'll grab a space in the open air, allowing you to observe in peace the comings and goings in the eye of the tourist hurricane.

Address Cafe Konditorei Fürst, Alter Markt and Brodgasse 13, A-5020 Salzburg, tel. +43 (0)662/8437590, www.original-mozartkugel.com | **Opening times** Mon–Sat 8am–9pm, Sun 9am–9pm; in winter up to 8pm | **Public transport** Buses no. 3, 5, 6, 8, 20, 25, 28, 160, 170, 270, stop Rathaus | **Tip** The sweet temptations from the house of Fürst are arranged in a particularly enticing way in the Ritzerbogen salesroom between Churfürststrasse and Universitätsplatz square.

75 __ The Plaque for August Bebel
The formative years of the German Socialist leader

Memorial plaques on many façades of the Old Town serve as reminders of fateful events or personalities who walked part of their life path in Salzburg. But sometimes a closer look at historical facts yields surprising results – as in the case of a stay by August Bebel (1840–1913), one of the founders of the German workers movement. His formative travels, what is known in German-speaking countries as the »Walz«, led him to the banks of the Salzach in 1859/60, where he offered his services to the Schatz woodturning establishment in Getreidegasse. His memorial in the »Schatz-Durchhaus« is a reminder that this shopping promenade was once home to craftsmen's workshops.

As Bebel was to write in his autobiography, the pay at the time was bad, as it was everywhere. He would have lived off rye bread and milk, apart from lunches taken with the Master craftsman. As an ascetic Prussian, Bebel had a hard time at the tavern tables. Although of Protestant faith, he was involved in the activities of the Catholic Journeymen's Union. In this spirit Bebel once took part in a pilgrimage to Maria Plain, as a barrel of beer was promised for afterwards.

Thanks to Bebel's memoirs, we have more anecdotes to give life to the meagre commemorative plaque. For instance, about Ludwig I of Bavaria, who had abdicated in 1848 because of the Lola Montez affair and was spending his summers at Leopoldskron Castle. One day he was helping a young boy to steal apples by throwing his cane up into the branches. He was promptly spotted by the farmer's wife who called out to the unknown apple stealer in the broadest dialect: »Ye old Rascal, ain't yer ashamed of yerself to help the boy steal apples!« The former king left the scene of the crime, and the next morning a servant appeared at the farmer's house to bring the woman a guilder with the remark that this was payment for the apples that the gentleman had beaten off the tree the previous day. That way she found out that the accomplice had been no less than King Ludwig.

In diesem Hause
arbeitete
deutsche Sozialistenführer
August Bebel
als Drechslergehilfe
1859 – 1860.

Address Schatz-Durchhaus, Getreidegasse 3/3a, A-5020 Salzburg | **Public transport**
Buses no. 3, 5, 6, 8, 20, 25, 28, 160, 170, 270, stop Rathaus (city hall) | **Tip** Café-Konditorei
Schatz is the best place to stock up on sweetmeats and gateaux.

76 The Punz Vegetable Stall

Wonder tomatoes on the Schranne market

Long Erwin, Black Prince, Green Zebra or Red Bull's Heart. They all share a sad tomato fate, having been pushed to the brink of extinction over the past decades. Because their yield wasn't big enough, because they had a colour that many consumers didn't appreciate, were not so easy to keep or transport perhaps.

However, this is not true everywhere. In Wals, the vegetable-growing dynasty of Punz-Hörmann has made it their mission to revive the tomato diversity of former times. Which is why you should be sure to visit the Martin Punz vegetable stand on the popular Schrannen market.

Punz's vegetable fields and greenhouses in Wals-Siezenheim serve as an experimental laboratory, while his stall behind St. Andrä Church is proof of the sheer variety of the tomato universe. A feast for the eyes expands in front of the tomato aficionado. Bright red giants sit next to delicate reddish-brown cherry tomatoes, the fruit shining yellow and orange in their boxes, piling up in bulging, vitamin-rich mounds. One thing is shared by the »exotic« fruit here: in both aroma and flavour they are very different from the products cultivated and optimised by agrochemical companies and sold in the supermarkets.

The experiment started a good ten years ago. Today, the slow food pioneer has about 60 rare types of tomato ready for selling in the spring; some 25 types are cultivated for fruit harvest in their own greenhouses.

The tomato festival starts in July and lasts until October, when the first frost sets. Business is going well, and those who find themselves in front of empty shelves at Schrannenmarkt can start planning the weekend shop.

On Saturdays, the tomato prodigy also puts in a guest appearance on the Grünmarkt at Universitätsplatz square.

Address Mirabellplatz, A-5020 Salzburg; the Punz-Hörmann vegetable stall is located to the back of the St. Andrä Church | **Opening times** Thu 6am–1pm | **Public transport** Buses no. 1, 2, 4, 3, 5, 6, 21, 22, 25, 32, 120, 130, 131, 140, 141, 150, 152, 154, stop Mirabellplatz | **Tip** The organ of St Andra is often played by students from the Mozarteum conservatorium. With a little luck, a visitor to the church might catch a free concert.

77__ The Puppet Theatre
Nowhere do the puppets dance more gracefully

When the curtain rises in Salzburg's puppet theatre, an extraordinary, poetic event is unveiled. The eye adapts to the stage opening, which is a little smaller than usual.

Music can be heard, and then the main protagonists float onto the stage: puppets masterfully led on strings, which are manoeuvred by marionette players. The figures, some 70 centimetres/27 inches tall, act to arias from Mozart's »Magic Flute« or the musical version of »The Sound of Music«. Onlookers soon forget that what they are seeing here are »only« puppets, rather than flesh and blood human beings.

The theatre is 100 years old. In the beginning, the team made a name for itself with Punch & Judy-type performances. From 1926 onwards, the repertoire was expanded with fairy tales and opera, performed using voiceovers and live music. Once the audio tape was invented, in the 1950s, the global career of the Salzburg Puppet Theatre took off. Tours of the US, South America and Europe earned the ensemble rave reviews for their poetic »Gesamtkunstwerk«.

Nothing is left to chance here. A director stages the pieces, while a choreographer works out the dance parts. The puppets are made in-house – from the wig to the shoe buckle. Only the heads are commissioned from sculptors.

The music is composed by renowned orchestras and soloists, and it is this musicality that makes the Salzburg puppets so unique. The illusion is perfected through the high art of the players.

Their dexterity and delicate skills lend the puppets feelings such as sadness, anger or happiness. A man who freezes, erupting with rage turns around in anger, a wolf stalking his prey – all this can be followed intuitively by the audience, whether young or old. The repertoire comprises, amongst others, five Mozart operas, Shakespeare's »Midsummer Night's Dream« and the children's opera »Peter and the Wolf«.

Address Salzburg Marionette Theatre, Schwarzstrasse 24, A-5020 Salzburg, tel. +43 (0)662/872406, www.marionetten.at | Opening times Information about the performances is available on the theatre homepage | Public transport Buses no. 1, 3, 4, 5, 6, 21, 22, 25, 27, 160, 170, stops Makartplatz or Theatergasse | Tip If you'd like to just get a taste we recommend the one-hour matinees. An exhibition of marionettes can be visited at Hohensalzburg Castle.

78__ The Rainberg Mountain
This urban mountain is »off limits« for two-legged creatures

»The Lost World« is the name of a novel published in 1912 by iconic British writer Sir Arthur Conan Doyle. In it he describes the exploration of a secret plateau in the South American jungle, which is said to still be inhabited by prehistoric creatures. A similarly inaccessible »Tepui« (table-top mountain), the Rainberg in the Riedenburg part of town, is shrouded in the aura of a »Lost World« too. No access, say all possible entrance points; barriers, jagged rock faces and seemingly impenetrable shrubbery underlining the fact that Salzburg's smallest mountain wants to be left alone.

For a long time, the Rainberg formed the centre of settlement activities in the Salzburg area. When the Romans, in around 15 BC, founded the settlement of Iuvavum where the Old Town is today, the area around the Rainberg became mainly agricultural. However, after the pastures were abandoned in the 20th century and the only stone quarry was closed off, nature started gaining the upper hand. The mountain ridge was taken over by forest and is today hidden by a dense cover of beeches, linden and other deciduous trees.

The steppe slope on the mountain's southwestern side is considered a special ecological area, offering valuable habitat to warmth-loving plants and animals.

Owlet moths, heath snails, numerous species of grasshoppers, as well as smooth snakes, find ideal conditions on this natural hot spot. Dyer's broom, speedwell, squincywort and other beauties stretch their blossoms skywards here. In order to avoid the bush cover taking over completely, in summer the slope is grazed by goats.

The Rainberg is a nature reserve, and since access was formally prohibited in 1955, few people have set foot on or explored the last foothill of the Mönchsberg. One of them was Peter Handke, who found a »savannah of freedom« in the heart of the city. However, he didn't write anything about prehistoric creatures.

Address Rainberg, A-5020 Salzburg (Riedenburg), between Sinnhubstrasse (south), Leopoldskronstrasse (west) and Rainbergstrasse (north) | **Public transport** Buses no. 21, 22, stop Sinnhubstrasse, Obus no. 1, 2, 4, stop Moosstrasse | **Tip** The best place for fine views of the Rainsberg is Mönchsberg. An rare chance to gain legal access to the Rainberg can sometimes be had during the »Week of Biodiversity« in late spring.

79__The Richterhöhe

A monument to a glaciologist

Glaciologists are always good for some excitement and media frenzy, whether they are predicting the disappearance of the alpine glaciers by the year 2050, or warning of the devastating consequences of the melting of the Greenland ice cap. But 100 or 150 years ago scientific engagement with the »eternal« ice in the high mountain regions of the Alps was still an exotic area of research. One of its pioneers was Eduard Richter (1847–1905), who worked in Salzburg for many years, giving his name to the Richterhöhe on Mönchsberg with its old fortification buildings.

Richter was one of the researchers whose early glacier measurements laid the foundations for important series of historical comparisons. The trigger for his investigations was provided by geodesic measurements, begun in the 1870s, on the Swiss Rhone glaciers. The geographer decided to organise similar measurements for the ice giants in the Eastern Alps.

Eventually, under Richter's leadership, a kind of encyclopedia of glaciers emerged, documenting the size of over 1,000 glaciers of the Eastern Alps.

Some of the ice giants were examined by the passionate mountaineer himself. Phenomena such as the dangerous advance of the Vernagtferner and Gurglerferner glaciers in the 17th and 18th centuries aroused Richter's interest and encouraged him to look for a connection between glacial variation and meteorological data such as the amount of precipitation.

In 1886, Richter was appointed to Graz University as Professor of Geography, while from 1898 to 1900 he headed the international glacier commission. Furthermore, the polymath also made a name for himself as a lake researcher, historian and Alpine Club president. Unveiled in 1907, the marble monument shows Eduard Richter, kitted out for a mountaineering jaunt, his gaze directed longingly towards the distance.

Eduard Richter *1847 †1905
dem begeisterten Alpenforscher
seine Freunde und Verehrer

Address Richterhöhe, Mönchsberg, A-5020 Salzburg | Public transport Buses no. 1, 4, 8, 22,
stop Herbert-von-Karajan-Platz, 20 minutes on foot via Toscanini-Hof and Clemens-
Holzmeister-Stiege; or via Mönchsberg Elevator from the Mönchsbergaufzug bus stop,
approx. 15 minutes on foot via Mönchsberg | Tip A few yards from the monument, a panel
display illustrates the majestic mountains to the south.

80 __ The Robert Jungk International Futures Library

Salzburg's progressive think tank

Prophets have always had a hard time of it, especially if their pronouncements are of the mythological naysaying Cassandra variety. The same holds true for Robert Jungk (1913–1994), who has entered the history books as one of the 20th century's major pioneers and futurologists. The campaign against nuclear energy and the arms race of the Cold War superpowers were the major subjects of the Berlin-born researcher, who started working out of Salzburg in 1971 and was awarded the »Right Livelihood Award«, the alternative Nobel Prize, in 1986. Today, the Robert-Jungk-Bibliothek fur Zukunftsfragen (JBZ) offers a platform for gauging the dangers and opportunities of »possible futures«, its influence extending far beyond Salzburg.

Since Jungk's death the spectrum of future risks has grown dramatically. Hardly a day goes by without headlines warning of imminent climate collapse, over-fished seas or other consequences of our exploitation of nature. This is accompanied by news on the effects of globalisation, dividing the world into camps of haves and ever more have-nots. If you'd like to find out more on any of these subjects, the library is equipped with 15,000 works as well as over 160 magazines, plus comprehensive information and associated data. For an initial overview, consult the library's own series of publications. Beyond its role in imparting knowledge, the JBZ also functions as a think tank.

With the help of symposiums, workshops and »future workshops« based on Jungk's ideas, the centre tries to make the future the subject of general public discourse. And those who find that steam is coming out of their brains from thinking so hard may want to do as Robert Jungk did and head off on a long walk to the Brunnhaus in the Nonntal Valley.

Address Robert-Jungk-Platz 1 (Imbergstrasse 2), A-5020 Salzburg, tel. +43 (0)0662/873206, www.jungk-bibliothek.at | Opening times Mon–Wed 9am–2pm, Thu 4–9pm | Public transport Buses no. 3, 5, 6, 7, 8, 20, 25, 28, 160, 170, stop Mozartsteg/Rudolfskai (changing across to the right-hand bank of the Salzach) or stop Mozartsteg/Imbergstrasse | Tip Worth a visit is the Jewish cemetery in Salzburg-Aigen, Uferstrasse 47, where Robert Jungk and his wife Ruth occupy a grave of honour placed here by the city of Salzburg.

81__ The Roof of the Rock Riding School

Finally in the dry after 90 years

A monumental stage with the escarped walls of the Mönchsberg rising dramatically behind, three floors of arcades carved into the rock, and an auditorium rising like an amphitheatre – for many guests of the Salzburg Festival, the »Felsenreitschule« is the most atmospheric of the performance spaces. The fact that for a long time it was also deemed to be its most problematic was down to the lack of proper roofing. The various provisional solutions thought up since the 1920s for the protection of festivalgoers – which at a later date also included the stage area – were not exactly the last word in construction. When rain hammered on the roof, the artists suffered as much as the visitors in the back rows, and for the whole winter the stage was more or less at the mercy of the elements.

Then the era arrived where retractable roofs were developed for American football stadiums and eventually even for the Centre Court at the time-honoured Wimbledon tennis club. Once these roofs had stood the technical test of time and found favour with the public, Salzburg began a new attempt at solving the roof question. Then, in 2010 the moment arrived, and heavy machinery rolled up at the Toscanini courtyard.

Since the completion of the technically ambitious modification, the Felsenreitschule finally boasts a simply constructed yet extremely efficient roof. If rain is announced, telescopic poles are extended to fit into recesses in the rock of Mönchsberg mountain. Mobile segments slide across each other – and hey presto! The construction is moved by electrical motors, silently and swiftly. The acoustics have improved, and one side effect of the renovation is two extra floors to accommodate the technology and staff. And as the musical enjoyment on offer at the Rock Riding School is now much improved, come rain or shine, the prices, ranging from 45 to 360 euros, seem a bit less painful.

Address Hofstallgasse 1, A-5020 Salzburg, tel. +43 (0)662/80450, www.salzburgerfest-spiele.at | Opening times Guided tours through the Festival venues daily 2pm, June and Sept also 3.30pm, July and Aug also 9.30am | Public transport Buses no. 1, 4, 8, 22, stop Herbert-von-Karajan-Platz | Tip Edmundsburg Castle on Mönchsberg is – assuming the roof is open – a good place from which to listen to rehearsals or performances in the Rock Riding School.

82__ The Rose Hill
Love is in the air

There's no shortage of places for couples in love in the city of Mozart; yet there can be few that arouse such romantic feelings as Rose Hill at the northern end of the Mirabellgarten. This small elevation occupies a mound sheltering what is left of the old St. Vital bastion from the time of the Thirty Years War, offering fantastic views of the World Heritage site of Salzburg.

Many visitors use the famous sight line across the baroque gardens towards Hohensalzburg Castle in the south as the start of their sightseeing programme. The myriad roses are an invitation to sit down on one of the benches and let the aroma of the flowers waft over you. Year after year the municipal gardeners bring Rose Hill and the other parts of the Mirabellgarten to life through their artful arrangements.

»Love is in the air, everywhere you look around«: for decades, Rose Hill has been a meeting point for the gay community, on balmy summer nights in particular. A love story also surrounds the graceful dancer amidst the flower beds and arrangements. This sculpture of a naked lady was created by the well-known Italian sculptor Giacomo Manzu (1908–1991).

In 1954, the Lombard artist travelled to Salzburg thanks to an initiative of Oskar Kokoschka, in order to share his expertise with young artists in the new summer academy at Hohensalzburg Castle. Initially, the sculptor faced a problem: there weren't many models, and even fewer managed to inspire him.

In the end the state theatre sent over members of its ensemble, resulting in a young prima ballerina called Inge Schabel posing for the artist. She soon became his favourite model and, one thing leading to another, the muse eventually turned into the wife of the great man. Since 1976, the sculpture immortalising her – the Dancer – has adorned this elevated viewpoint.

Address Mirabellpark / Kurpark, access from Mirabellplatz, A-5020 Salzburg | Opening times Freely accessible all year round | Public transport Buses no. 1, 2, 4, 3, 5, 6, 21, 22, 25, 32, 120, 130, 131, 140, 141, 150, 152, 154, stop Mirabellplatz | Tip Salzburg Cathedral's »Gate of Love« was also created by Giacomo Manzu. An easy-to-navigate Mirabellgarten info pack is available for download at:
www.stadt-salzburg.at / pdF / mirabellgarten__geschichte_und_gegenwart__2009.pdf

83__ The Salzburg Bull

Rise and shine, this mechanical organ used to roar

Imagine a place where »Big Brother« orders when the citizens should rise from their beds and when they should sleep again. And where aural means are used for this purpose, transmitting commands that can be heard everywhere. Salzburg once had such a contraption: the »Salzburg Bull«.

Behind this moniker lies the world's oldest still functioning mechanical organ. Its construction dates back to Archbishop Leonhard von Keutschach. In the first years of the 16th century, he had a large mechanical organ built in a wooden alcove on the exterior castle wall, consisting of a wind box, bellows and 135 pipes. At the request of the highest ranking Salzburger, the instrument would kick into action at four o'clock in the morning and send its shrill F-major notes across the town once more at seven in the evening, after the prayer bell. In a report from a later era we find the nice phrasing that the archbishop was using this to »sound the retreat and tagreveille with his beloved Salzburgers«, tagreveille being the traditional waking call for newlyweds.

It is not known how seriously the citizens would have taken the exhortations of the organ, which became known as the Salzburg Bull for its much-amplified, »roaring« sounds.

Around 1560, the instrument was complemented by a barrel organ, which was also able to play a few musical set pieces. Two hundred years later, during a further reconstruction, the musical element finally gained the upper hand over the alarm function. The current repertoire of the barrel organ – today equipped with over 200 pipes – comprises nearly ten melodies, with the characteristic chords starting and ending the pieces.

From Palm Sunday to 31 October, the Salzburg Bull rings out daily at 7am, 11am and 6pm after the carillon. The fact that he can hardly be heard now in some parts of the Old Town is for a very simple reason: the roar of a bull is no match for the roar of the traffic.

Address Hohensalzburg Castle, at the Krautturm tower, A-5020 Salzburg, tel. +43 (0)662/ 84243011, www.festung-salzburg.at | **Opening times** May–Sept 9am–7pm, Oct–April 9.30am–5pm; the audio tours at the Castle allow a glimpse of the instrument | **Public transport** Festungsbahn cable car, from Festungsgasse 4 | **Tip** A gem in the castle yard is the Matthäus Lang cistern, erected in 1539 by Venetian master builders and surrounded by a diamond mesh.

84 The Salzburg Panorama
The whole of Salzburg in one autumn day in 1825

Some artworks are so daring they take your breath away. One of those is the Salzburg panorama created by Johann Michael Sattler (1786–1847).

In 1824, the painter took up a suggestion made by Emperor Franz I, went to the fortress and started to fix the outline of the town, its buildings and surroundings from five different angles and in comprehensive detail. Next he arranged for two colleagues to help him fix the 360-degree panorama in oil on a huge canvas of just under 26 metres/85 feet in length and five metres/16 feet in height. When Sattler presented his panoramic painting at Easter 1829 in a pavilion on the square that today is called Makartplatz, he gained instant fame.

There had been nothing like it in the entire Danube monarchy. The Sattlers packed their dismountable painting onto their houseboat and toured through Europe over the following ten years. In Germany, Belgium, France, Holland and Scandinavia the diorama accomplished invaluable tourism PR.

Nearly 200 years later, a dedicated museum tells the story of the world's only remaining giant city panorama. Visitors can use telescopes mounted on a platform to zoom themselves into the world of 1825 and lose themselves in countless details. The circular painting shows Salzburg in bright colours on a sunny autumn afternoon, with all the church clocks set to 4pm.

In front of a house in Leopoldskron, washing flaps in the wind. Cows are being led to drink at the Salzach River, then still running its natural course. There are no railway tracks and few buildings marring the townscape. The Panorama Museum provides an insight into day-to-day life in early 19th-century Salzburg that couldn't be conveyed by ten books, while installations document the changes since Sattler's time. This is a journey back in time that you will never grow tired of.

Address Panorama Museum, Residenzplatz 9, A-5010 Salzburg, tel. +43 (0)662/620808730, www.salzburgmuseum.at | Opening times Daily 9am–5pm | Public transport Buses no. 3, 5, 6, 7, 8, 20, 25, 28, 160, 170, stop Mozartsteg/Rudolfskai | Tip The museum occasionally displays dioramas by the Sattler family, for instance, views of New York. Hohensalzburg Castle shows reproductions of the preliminary designs for the major Salzburg panoramic painting.

85 __ Salzburg's Smallest House

Just 1.42 metres/4.65 feet? No reason to suffer
from an inferiority complex!

So small and yet still a house – this is probably the first thought of most people when standing in front of the building on Alter Markt 10a and letting their gaze roam across the facade. Stretching out your arms would cover the whole thing from one end to the other. With a width of just 1.42 metres/4.65 feet, the house is a Salzburg curiosity.

It was built in the mid-19th century when the decision was made, apparently for lack of space, to build along a tiny lane just a few yards across. Considering the fact that commercial space is at a premium in the heart of the Old Town, it was a decision that kind of makes sense.

One glance is enough to make it clear why the little house doesn't boast six storeys like its neighbours: a staircase would swallow up far too much space. The architect instead decided on a version between one-and-a-half and two storeys. As it is, with a tiny attic room any average person would run the risk of continually banging their head.

Still, there's really no reason for it to feel inferior, as there are a number of features worth looking out for. Take the splendid gargoyle, half dragon, half demon, adorning the steep roof. Above the mythical creatures, graceful flying buttresses maintain the distance to overpowering neighbours. To the left you have a luxury boutique, to the right a watchmaker flogs his trendy products to the people. And in fact, the squeezed little house itself boasts an interesting interior. A fancy French jeweller, who doesn't need that much exhibition space for his precious things, rents Salzburg's smallest house. Mirrors and clever lighting let the jewels shine on this very effective stage. Jewellery and other »must-haves« await potential clients on red velvet, but the sparkling treasures may only be viewed by one or two people at the most.

Address Alter Markt 10a, A-5020 Salzburg | Public transport Buses no. 3, 5, 6, 8, 20, 25, 28, 160, 170, 270, stop Rathaus | Tip The Old Prince Archbishop Court Pharmacy, located diagonally across at Alter Markt 6, boasts a splendid original interior.

86__ The Schlapp Stüberl
»Schlipp, schlapp, schlorum« and other rituals

»Schlipp, schlapp, schlorum basilorum, in catacombis et ubique locorum« – what sounds like a nursery rhyme in primitive Latin is actually the motto of one of Salzburg's oldest associations: the Schlapp Society. This society holds its meetings in the Augustiner Braustübl Mülln and is the only of the over 120 regular one to have sat there for so long to now be entitled to get together in a dedicated room, the Schlapp-Stüberl.

The patina and furnishings make it clear that tradition is valued here. Wood-panelled walls, old cupboards, and the odd chair with the ergonomic standards of the Biedermeier era provide a rustic setting for the get-togethers.

The Schlapp Brothers have been meeting since 1859. The name is said to go back to a card game from Italy, the rules of which have been lost in the mists of time. What happens during the meetings is a secret – at least in a tongue-in-cheek kind of way, with proceedings falling under the Schlapp Oath.

However, you can safely assume that it'll mainly involve the same as other regular get-togethers in the Braustübl Mülln: cosy conviviality and animated discussion around a substantial quantity of beer. Possibly the rituals distinguishing this get-together might be a bit more sophisticated though. You only need to listen at the door to find that a »Schlipp« is uttered before the beer mugs are banged together.

And there's another idiosyncrasy that distinguishes Stüberl and Co.: new members have to bring a coat-of-arms to the society when they join. The emblem has to portray a rebus (a heraldic picture puzzle) involving clues to the name and profession of the bearer. Thus, the coat-of-arms of co-founder Franz Stelzhamer – who wrote the words of the Upper Austrian regional anthem – features a lyre. Eight stars are arranged above, and the instrument is flanked by a hammer amongst other things. Enjoy the guessing game!

Address Augustiner Brau Kloster Mülln, Lindhofstrasse 7, A-5020 Salzburg, tel. +43 (0)662/431246, www.augustinerbier.at | **Opening times** Braustübl for non-regulars: daily 3pm–11pm, Sat, Sun and public holidays 2.30–11pm (ask staff if you can have a peek inside the Stüberl) | **Public transport** Buses no. 7, 10, 20, 21, 24, 27 (on weekdays direct connection to the train station), 28, stop Landeskrankenhaus regional hospital; S-Bahn S2 and S3, stop Mülln-Altstadt | **Tip** Another place exuding plenty of flair is the Braugasthof Krimpelstatter in Müllner Hauptstrasse 31. Things are quieter in this classic Salzburg hostelry than they sometimes get at the Augustiner Bräu.

87 __ The »Sound of Music« bus terminal

Family Trapp fans of the world unite!

They reckon that the »Edelweiss« song is the Austrian national anthem and »Schnitzel with Noodles« the country's favourite dish. We are talking about those visitors to Salzburg from abroad who formed their image of Austria mainly from the 1965 Hollywood movie »The Sound of Music«. Its subject is the extraordinary tale of the Trapp family from Salzburg who captured American hearts with their songs.

The story begins in the mid-1920s when nun-to-be Maria Augusta Kutschera is sent to the widowed Georg Ritter von Trapp in order to help him educate his seven children. Marriage soon follows and, recognising the children's musical potential, Maria von Trapp forms a professional concert troupe. Not wanting anything to do with the Nazis, the Trapps move to the US in 1938 and become a roaring success as the »Trapp Family Singers«.

However, the story's final step towards cult status is when Hollywood takes hold of the material. To this day, »The Sound of Music« defines the (kitschy) image of Salzburg in North and South America, as well as in Asia, supposedly gaining 300,000 visitors a year to Austria. Many of whom book the »Original Sound of Music Tour – as seen in the Movie«, put on by the operator who once chauffeured Julie Andrews, Christopher Plummer and the rest of the acting troupe through Salzburg. Colourful plastic cows at the bus terminal start things off, while the buses are decorated with large likenesses of the stars. And off we go! Four hours are enough to cover the whole »SoM« universe. From Mirabell Palace via Leopoldskron and Hellbrunn, the trip heads for Mondsee Lake, 30 kilometres/18.5 miles away, which in the film provides the backdrop for the Trapp wedding. Some fans turn up in traditional dresses at the bus terminal and sway rhythmically through the tour, which is only available in English.

Address Mirabellplatz/corner Hubert-Sattler-Gasse, A-5020 Salzburg, tel. +43 (0)662/ 874029, www.panoramatours.com | Opening times Start 9.30am and 2pm | Public transport Buses no. 2, 4, 3, 5, 6, 21, 22, 25, 32, 120, 130, 131, 140, 141, 150, 152, 154, stop Mirabellplatz | Tip The family's former residence, Villa Trapp in Traunstrasse 34 in the Aigen part of town, is today managed as a bed and breakfast (A-5026 Salzburg, tel. +43 (0)662/630860, www.villa-trapp.com).

88 The Spirits Shop
From A for Allasch to Z for Zirbenschnaps

If there was an equivalent to the Slow Food movement in the field of spirits, the products sold at the tiny Sporer spirits shop would be a leading candidate. This family-run concern has developed great expertise in the production of high-strength liqueurs, some of them quite exotic.

On the shelves here you will find Allasch, for instance, a semi-sweet cumin liqueur which is practically impossible to source elsewhere. Recently a beer liqueur from the olden days was resurrected, while another popular product is the mocca liqueur brewed from real filter coffee. A liqueur with the Sporer seal of approval cannot be too sweet or too laden with spices, and artificial aromas are not welcome. The alcohol content tends to be above that of traditional liqueurs. Some batches comprise only 200 to 300 litres per year and just under half of the 40 products here are liqueurs.

The range also includes brandies and schnapps, such as the resinous Zirbenschnaps, made from tender Swiss pines cones marinated in grain brandy.

The recipe for the orange punch, a perennial favourite at Advent time in Salzburg, dates back to 1927. Oranges and lemons and various kinds of rum find their way into this fruity concentrate, but the exact recipe is kept a closely-guarded family secret.

As is the one for the house blend, which was first used as a digestive following a lavish meal for Sporer customers in the 1950s. All they will reveal is that 19 different kinds of berries, herbs and roots make up the fine semi-sweet herbal liqueur (38 per cent alcohol). The products are staged to great effect across just 38 square metres. The eye-catching feature of the shop is the double row of 18 wooden barrels serving as containers for rum tea, other spirits and the house vinegar.

On request you can have your favourite drink poured directly from the barrel into your own bottle.

Address Spirituosen Sporer, Getreidegasse 39, A-5020 Salzburg, tel. +43 (0)662/845431, www.sporer.at | Opening times Mon–Fri 9.30am–7pm, Sat 8.30am–5pm | Public transport Buses no. 1, 4, 8, 22, stop Herbert-von-Karajan-Platz | Tip Every Wednesday, a tasting session of Austrian specialities takes place. The entrance to the building features four historic doorbell pull-cables.

89__The Stefan Zweig Centre
Late recognition for a great European

Anna Meingast is the name of the woman who made an important contribution to a museum that was long overdue in Salzburg. For many years, she worked as a secretary to Stefan Zweig, who lived in the city on the Salzach between 1919 and 1934 and left it following a house raid by police serving the Austrofascist state (another reason was his marriage, which was in tatters). Meingast was to remain Zweig's confidant in Salzburg.

Decades later, letters written by the author and personal items appeared, documenting Zweig's creative work in the city and in the first years of his exile. The collection became part of the exhibition at the Stefan Zweig Centre Salzburg, inaugurated in 2008 in the Edmundsburg building.

In five chapters, the exhibition documents the stages of Zweig's life and his literary work up to his famous book of memoirs, »The World of Yesterday«, which was only published after the author's suicide in 1942 in Brazil. Original letters, photographs, film posters and many other exhibits paint a picture of a man who stood up for his ideals of pacifism and the cohesion of Europe following World War One. Also on display is the typewriter used by Meingast to type the correspondence for Zweig. With blank cheques bearing Zweig's signature, which his secretary had permission to cash, the author would provide for his long journeys.

The Stefan Zweig Centre is financed by the city, the region and the University of Salzburg. It can be found on the »other« city mountain, which Zweig didn't inhabit – the Mönchsberg. A comprehensive library gives researchers the opportunity to carry out scientific work on Zweig and his time and to consult original editions. The Centre's programme also features lectures, readings and scientific conferences on the work of famous writers, as well as on European literary and cultural history.

Address Edmundsburg, Mönchsberg 2, A-5020 Salzburg, tel. +43 (0)662/80447641, www.stefan-zweig-centre-salzburg.at | Opening times Mon, Wed, Thu, Fri 2–4pm, phone ahead for guided tours | Public transport Buses no. 1, 4, 8, 22, stop Herbert-von-Karajan-Platz, 10 minutes on foot via Toscanini-Hof and Clemens-Holzmeister-Stiege | Tip Literature lovers might like to stock up on Salzburg reading matter in the Höllrigl bookshop, Sigmund-Haffner-Gasse 10, or in the Rupertus bookshop, Dreifaltigkeitsgasse 12.

90__The Stefan Zweig Villa
A writers' refuge on Kapuzinerberg

When the snowflakes are swirling, the Kapuzinerberg is in danger of slipping off Salzburg's map. That's when you need either a good pair of boots or to be a good driver, in order to tackle the steep ascent from Linzer Gasse.

For its residents, these external circumstances can also provide relief from unwanted or all-too-frequent visits. And the author Stefan Zweig (1881–1942) might well have moved to the Kapuzinerberg for a calming counterpoint to his tiring public life.

For 15 years Zweig lived in the 17th-century Paschinger Schlossl, as it was called, which he had purchased in 1919 in a desolate state of disrepair. This is where he would receive famous personalities from Arturo Toscanini and James Joyce to Thomas Mann and H. G. Wells. On the terrace he would work on his essays and historical biographies on Joseph Fouche and Marie Antoinette, which were to make him one of the most-translated writers of his time.

On a regular basis he would make his the way down into the city to hold court in Café Bazar or to read the papers.

Zweig himself called the yellow manor house his »pushing-off point to Europe«. In 1934, the fascists took power in Austria. Following a raid on his house to find arms, Zweig left Salzburg, burned all bridges with the place and arranged for his estate to be sold.

With this, the Zweig Villa too slipped off the literary map – to this day. Walls, fences, hedges and Keep Out signs close off the estate hermetically on all sides.

Today's owners don't want Zweig's former residence to become a pilgrimage site for literary tourists and sightseers. There isn't even a memorial plaque.

Today, only the Stefan-Zweig-Weg street and a bust erected next to the Capuchin monastery in the 1980s serve to remind passers-by of the great European and pacifist.

Address Kapuzinerberg 5 / Stefan-Zweig-Weg, A-5020 Salzburg | **Public transport** Buses no. 1, 3, 4, 5, 6, 21, 22, 25, 27, 160, 170, stops Theatergasse or Makartplatz, 5 minutes on foot to the ascent of Kapuzinerberg from the Franziskuspforte gate in Linzer Gasse | **Tip** The door at the foot of the garden was a present from the poet's first wife, Friderike von Winternitz, who designed it herself. Another very charming way onto the Kapuzinerberg leads via Imbergstiege.

91__Steingasse

Salzburg City without make-up

If you're a bit tired of all the baroque façades and pretty views in Salzburg, head into Steingasse on the right-hand banks of the Salzach to discover a more unvarnished version of the city. Take just a few steps from the Platzl, and you'll see the houses huddling closer together, their façades becoming ever more grey and drab, their shadows running deeper.

Potters, tanners, linen weavers and other craftsmen who depended on the waters of the nearby river, would once be found working below the slopes of the Capuchin mountain. Their labours were accompanied by the rattling of the horse-and-carts rolling through the canyon of lanes on what was traditionally Salzburg's most important north-south link.

It was in the year 1792 that Joseph Mohr was born in Steingasse, as the out-of-wedlock child of a poor weaver. The hangman offered to be godfather to the child, in an attempt to improve his public image. Long after his death, Mohr would become famous as the composer of the »Silent Night, Holy Night« Christmas carol, but by that time his trail was already getting cold.

Today, experts no longer believe that the building next to the Imbergstiege (Steingasse 9), marked by a memorial plaque, was in fact Mohr's birthplace.

Continuing along to Steingasse 31, probably the historically correct address, and onto Äußerer Stein, the modest little lane reveals its contradictory character. On the one hand, with its bends, it submits to the rocky authority of the Capuchin mountain, while on the other it offers resistance, going on the attack. So, in their desire for more residential space, the Steingasse residents started building into the mountain. Their urge for light and air is reflected in the small terraces and balconies high above. In contrast to the Äußerer Stein, the odd piece of modern architecture has smuggled itself into the medieval picture.

Address Steingasse 9, A-5020 Salzburg | Public transport Buses no. 3, 5, 6, 7, 8, 20, 25, 28, 160, 170, stops Mozartsteg/Imbergstrasse or Äußerer Stein (heading into the city) or Mozartsteg/Rudolfskai (heading out of the city) | Tip If you'd like to escape the hustle and bustle of Salzburg's city centre for a while, we recommend a stroll from Linzer Gasse to Äußerer Stein.

92__ The Stiegl World of Beer
Beer history served with beer-related experiments

It is often claimed that whole worlds separate beer and women. However, it wasn't always like this. Did you realise that beer brewing, in the Salzburg region at least, was historically a woman's affair, and that until the 17th century many women would have brought a brewing copper into the marriage as a dowry? It is insights like this that make a visit to Stiegl Brauwelt in the Maxglan part of town so worthwhile.

Today, Stiegl is the biggest private brewery in Austria. Since its foundation in 1492, a good number of items have been accumulated and are now presented in style under the patronage of Gambrinus, legendary king of beer. The collection comprises magnificent beer mugs, original tools from times past, guild symbols, the world's tallest »beer tower« and plenty more. The tower of the former maltworks offers a fitting backdrop to a beer history told with panache. For instance, it seems that the brewing process was anything but an exact science in the olden days. With over half of the concoction something would go wrong, giving rise to the German expression »Hopfen und Malz verloren«, i.e. where hops and malt are lost, it's a hopeless case.

At this interactive brewery visitors can watch the establishment's top creative minds in action. The special beers produced by the microbrewery include the »Wildshuter Sortenspiel« (selection), featuring ancient grains such as spelt and emmer wheat, or creations with herbs. At Christmas, honey might enter the equation too. The message is clear: beer is anything but boring, from the artfully designed labels through to the fact that the »house beers« are only available for a few weeks at a time. So go for it while you can! The brewery also tries to appeal to more delicate palates with lighter beers and cocktails.

In the Paracelsus Stube restaurant, sophisticated culinary art and beer come together in harmony – anyone for honey beer tiramisu…?

Address Stiegl Brauwelt, Brauhausstrase 9, A-5020 Salzburg (Maxglan), tel. +43 (0)662/ 83871492, www.stiegl.at | Opening times Sept–June daily 10am–5pm, July and Aug 10am–7pm | Public transport Obus no.1, 8, stop Brauhausstrasse | Tip Local tour guide Martina Gyuroka offers an interesting beer walk through Salzburg. Contact her through www.salzburg-bierguide.at, tel. +43 (0)664/1456250.

93__ The Stieglkeller
Pub culture with great views

A sign in Festungsgasse saying »Nur 60 Schritte« and pointing towards the Stieglkeller pub, promises imminent salvation for thirsty visitors. The beer gardens on the terraces of the slope below the castle offer splendid views of the Old Town. Here, the domes of the cathedral are at eye level, church towers seem close enough to touch, and the hill crouching opposite is the Kapuzinerberg. All this atmosphere just heightens the anticipation of the freshly pulled amber nectar.

The beginnings of the Stieglkeller go back to the year 1820, when the then owner of the Stieglbrau started using the rooms of Festungsgasse no. 206 as a storage cellar.

The foaming heritage drink was supposed to be kept at a constant temperature by slabs of ice carted in and God's blessings, indicated by the small wall altars in the cellar rooms with their crucifixes. In 1840, the terraces above, which had previously served fortification purposes, were extended for the first time, with the so-called »Geniedirektion« in charge of the building permits. In the »beer happy years« preceding the First World War, when annual beer consumption in Salzburg reached a staggering 200 litres per person (the current Austrian figure is approx. 109 litres), the Stieglkeller was the most popular pub in Salzburg.

Today, the cellar is still a popular meeting place, bringing in the punters with heritage and home cooking. The beer garden, laid out in terraces, is more of a summertime proposition, but this large-scale beer temple also offers halls and nooks with seating for some 1200 people.

The snugs exude a cosy aura, as does the large hall with its wooden barrel vault. From here, a staircase takes you up steeply to the Bishop's Gallery, an arcaded balcony. An advance reservation at festival time might allow you, with a little luck, to listen to the Jedermann calls while sipping a cool beer.

Address Festungsgasse 10, A-5020 Salzburg | **Opening times** March–Jan daily 11am–midnight | **Public transport** Obus no. 1, 3, 4, 5, 6, 7, 8, stops Rathaus, Mozart-steg | **Tip** The route to the Stieglkeller via Festungsgasse leads you past St Peter's cemetery, which features the tomb of Salzburg's »beer poet« Otto Pflanzl (1865–1943)

94_ The Stiftsarmstollen Tunnel

Explore the heart of the Almkanal on foot

The Stiftsarmstollen is one of the most unusual destinations in Salzburg. The tunnel forms the heart of the Almkanal, which has provided Salzburg with water from the mountains south of the city since medieval times. The only opportunity to view the 400-metre/over 1310-feet long shaft is as part of a guided tour during the »Almabkehr« descent in September, when maintenance work is done on the widely branched system. Below the »Mayor's Hole«, this branch of the canal disappears into the mountain. So don your wellies, turn on your torch, and prepare to enter the belly of Salzburg.

The construction of the Stiftsarmstollen (1136–1143) is considered the crowning achievement in the art of medieval engineering. Using the simplest means, workers drove the shaft through the rock at the narrowest point between the castle mound and Mönchsberg on behalf of the cathedral chapter and St. Peter's monastery. They met with the most varied rock formations, from the easy to work conglomerate rock to hard dolomite, which helps to explain why what is probably the oldest water-bearing shaft in Central Europe is only 1.60 metres/5.2 feet high in places and features a number of curves.

There are astonishing sights down here. In the first few yards you meet light-shy spiders that build their webs on the wet rock. Gothic pointed arches and other vaulted forms provide clues as to in which era certain sections were restored. Mini stalactites shine in the torchlight; a tomb slab dragged into the shaft for repair purposes is visible. Another slab, made from Adnet marble, shows the contours of a fossilised ammonite. Below the castle cable-car, where you can see daylight again, the shaft branches off further.

In the area of the Old Town, the water of the Almkanal is today used mainly for cooling purposes and for generating energy. And on the way back, remember to keep your head down again!

Address Brunnhausgasse / corner Hans-Sedlmayr-Weg, A-5020 Salzburg | Opening times
For the »Almabkehr« in September, information on guided tours on the site | Public
transport Buses no. 5, 25, stop Erzabt-Klotz-Strasse | Tip It's worth trying to catch the
Almkanal exhibition in the exit area of the cable-car (access also from the jewellery shop
next door).

95__ The Stone Terrace

Where Tom Cruise posed with Cameron Diaz

From the terrace of Hotel Stein you have the whole of Salzburg lying at your feet. The gaze wanders across the green Salzach River and comes to rest on the World Heritage city's skyline of church steeples, before making its way across the walls of the castle to Mönchsberg and the Untersberg in the background. Of course, the tourism people are happy when Hollywood stars such as Tom Cruise or Cameron Diaz can be seen in the foreground.

But let's start at the beginning: the occasion for the appearance of these two was the publicity campaign for the action movie »Knight and Day«. In the film, Tom Cruise plays an agent who is led to the banks of the Salzach in the course of a tug-of-war surrounding a limitless source of energy. Possibly he might have enjoyed a box seat on the city while haring across the roofs of Steingasse during a night-time chase.

In any case, when the film had its world premiere in June 2010, the movie couple took a private jet to Salzburg to pose in the seventh floor of the hotel for the gathered media. Air kisses here, little waves there, a barrage of flashes going off everywhere – and the whole PR spectacle, showing Salzburg's most resplendent side, was broadcast by global TV stations and Internet platforms. Priceless publicity is the technical term for this kind of thing.

The »Steinterrasse« is a hip place to meet friends, to take a drink in the evening, to see and be seen. Little wonder then that the trendy meeting place on the right-hand banks of the Salzach has caught the attention of more film makers. In the movie version of the thriller by Wolf Haas, »Silentium«, private detective Brenner, played by Josef Hader, is cut down in chilling style by his boss on the »Steinterrasse«. He has no time for Salzburg nightlife or a drink at the bar.

A word of advice to all actors whose script demands that uncomfortable things befall them in this place: come back, enjoy a cappuccino or a cocktail and soak up this panorama in peace and quiet!

Address Hotel Stein, Giselakai 3–5, A-5020 Salzburg, tel. +43 (0)662 / 8743460, www.hotelstein.at | Opening times Terrace from 3pm | Public transport Buses no. 3, 5, 6, 8, 20, 25, 28, 160, 170, 270, stop Rathaus (city hall) | Tip For cinematic art beyond Hollywood blockbusters, head for »Das Kino« cinema next door (Giselakai 11).

96 The »Stumbling Stones« at the former »gypsy camp«

A dark chapter in Salzburg's history

The former swampland of Leopoldskron Moor in the southwest of the city is a popular recreational space. Cyclists and locals out for a stroll move along the Glan creek, which is spanned by several small bridges. But few of them know that one of the darkest chapters in Salzburg's history was written here. Those looking a bit closer around the Glan Bridge, at the intersection of Schwarzgrabenweg and Kräutlerweg, will notice the »Stolpersteine« - which translates as »stumbling stones« - embedded in the asphalt. They are there as a reminder of the fate of the people held in the former »gypsy camp« of Salzburg-Maxglan.

In September 1940, the Nazis interned 213 Sinti (a Romani group) in this hastily erected camp. The prisoners were subjected to inhuman treatment, unimaginable hygienic conditions and forced labour over the following two-and-a-half years. In April 1943, the survivors were deported and all but a few were murdered, the majority of them in Auschwitz-Birkenau. Today, nothing is left of the camp. Even finding the exact spot was difficult, which probably had much to do with the lack of public interest in the post-war years.

As part of the »Stolpersteine« project by German artist Gunter Demnig, which has found international resonance, brass tiles were sunk into the ground near the former camp between 2007 and 2009. They recall the names of the children born in captivity and murdered in Auschwitz. For instance, one of the stones reads (in translation): »AGATHE HERZENBERGER/BORN 1941/IN MAXGLAN CAMP/DEPORTED 1943/AUSCHWITZ/MURDERED 21/07/1943«. The names of the 17 children are intended to represent the 170 camp inmates deported in the year 1943. A sculpture too serves as an additional reminder of the fate suffered by the Sinti community.

Address Schwarzgrabenweg/Kräutlerweg, A-5020 Salzburg (Leopoldskron-Moos); the »Stolpersteine« memorial site is located on the right-hand banks of the Glan creek, right beside the bridge | **Public transport** Bus no. 27, stop Kräutlerweg | **Tip** This destination is easily integrated into a bike tour in the southwest of Salzburg. Heading out of the city, the Moosstrasse will take you to Schwarzgrabenweg, whereupon you can explore the Leopolds-kroner Moos along the Glan-Treppelweg and carry on cycling to Fürstenbrunn.

97__The Stupa
Buddhist source of energy power plant on Mönchsberg

Anyone hiking in the Salzburg mountains will sooner or later encounter the colourful pennants fluttering in the wind, evidence of the Buddhist philosophy of some Alpinists.

Even so, seeing the stupa on the Mönchsberg, which was inaugurated in autumn 2011, was a little surprising to many locals. Rising from a clearing up to a height of four metres/13 feet, it offers a view of Hohensalzburg Castle.

A stepped granite base runs up to a golden pinnacle, while pennants in white, red, yellow, blue and green only strengthen its exotic aura.

Its erection created some wonderment as normally it's extremely difficult to obtain a building permit on the Mönchsberg. Yet technically a building can be accessed – which is not the case for this Buddhist symbol of enlightenment and peace. So the building of the so-called Enlightenment Stupa only required an exemption permit, and the city was happy to support the initiative suggested by Salzburg's Diamond Way Buddhism community.

When erecting a stupa, nothing is left to chance. The spot on Mönchsberg was chosen personally by a top-level Master.

Following a precisely prescribed ceremony, the stupa was filled with thousands of relics, mantra rolls and Buddhist texts, grouped around a Tree of Life, and then sealed.

These are all important conditions for the stupa to fulfill its purpose: to work as a source of energy for everyone's benefit. It does that both by virtue of its form as well as the »jewels« kept inside. So if this stupa does help in leading people to their inner force that has to be good.

And may all those who don't buy into this achieve greater balance and inner peace, simply through walking or experiencing nature on Mönchsberg.

Address Mönchsberg, A-5020 Salzburg; discover the stupa via Clemens-Holzmeister-Stiege, Dr.-Herbert- Klein-Weg and Oskar-Kokoschka-Weg to the »Buffet Richterhöhe«; 80 metres/87 yards north, on an unmarked walking trail, www.stupa-salzburg.at | Opening times The stupa is freely accessible. | Public transport Mönchsberg Elevator from bus stop Mönchsbergaufzug, some 15 minutes on foot | Tip Take a stop at »Buffet Richterhöhe« to let the encounter sink in and replenish your strength for the continuation of the Mönchs-berg tour.

98 The Theatre of Stone

Where opera history was written in Hellbrunn

People sometimes forget that Salzburg was a centre of European music long before Mozart's strokes of genius and aeons before the Salzburg Festival, staged for the first time only in 1920. An important site in terms of this musical »prehistory« is the theatre of stone on Hellbrunn Mountain. This rock stage was born from a quarry, which provided the construction material for the Hellbrunn royal pleasure palace in the southern part of town 400 years ago. The artistically-minded Markus Sittikus, who spent a fortune on musical extravaganzas and masquerades, recognised the potential of this hole in the mountain as an atmospheric performance venue. On 31 August 1617, a few months before the Thirty Years War was to sweep across Central Europe, the archbishop issued invitations to an extravagant spectacle: a performance of the »L'Orfeo« opera by Claudio Monteverdi. There were plenty of »Ahs« and »Ohs« when the singers and actors appeared on stage via hidden entrances and disappeared again the same way – just like Orpheus, who descends into the underworld in order to win back his beloved Eurydice.

The event is commemorated on a memorial plaque as the »first opera performance on German soil«. Whatever the truth of this, it was certainly at least the first open-air opera performance in Central Europe. Today, the theatre, half sunken into the conglomerate rock, half hewn out of same, presents itself as an enchanted place off the beaten tourist track. It only takes a little imagination to spy a faun, a nymph or other mythological creatures in the shade of the bushes and trees; their marble brothers and sisters populate the nearby castle park. Light, water and stage technology are unknown in this forgotten theatre.

And this means that the only time you'll hear music is when the »Salzburger Volksliedwerk« folksong association invites people to the »Hellbrunner Volksliedsingen« singalong for the Assumption of the Virgin Mary (15 August).

Address Schlosspark Hellbrunn, Fürstenweg 37, A-5020 Salzburg, tel. +43 (0)662/8203720. The route to the rock theatre leads via the Schlosspark (free access), requiring shoes with a good grip | **Opening times** All year round | **Public transport** Bus no. 25 from main train station, stop Fürstenweg | **Tip** Located half-way, the small Monatsschlössl palace presents a collection of Salzburg popular art that is worth seeing.

99 The Thomas Bernhard Memorial Plaque

A love-hate relationship that made literary history

Thomas Bernhard (1931–1989) has entered Austrian literary history as the writer who was perhaps the most merciless in dealing with his home country. Bernhard's relationship with Austria is often described as one of love and hate in equal measure. The author reserved particular vitriol for Salzburg, where he spent more than a dozen years of his life from 1943 onwards. It may have been the difficult conditions – poverty, failure at school, family entanglements and a severe lung disease – which helped to create a deep dislike for the city that would inspire legendary tirades decades later. »Salzburg«, as he raged in his autobiographical novella »Die Ursache« (The Reason, 1975), »is a perfidious façade used by the world to incessantly paint its mendacity and behind which everything creative and every creator has to shrivel, decay and die. In truth, my hometown is a deathly disease …« collected in the 1985 memoir »Gathering Evidence«.

In terms of style, some of these passages are sublime, but unsurprisingly, Salzburgers were not entirely happy with being insulted in this way. Still, it's possible that without Salzburg as the place to grind his axe, this »Master of Exaggeration«, as he was once called, would never have reached the lofty literary heights that made his stage plays highlights of the Salzburg Festival in the 1970s and 80s. Under the direction of Claus Peymann, some of his most successful works, such as »The Ignoramus and the Madman« (1972) and »Histrionics« (1985), were first staged at Salzburg's Landestheater, which he had castigated as a »funfair of Dilettantism« just a few years previously. There would usually be some kind of commotion – but Bernhard saw that very excitement as an integral part of the »Salzburg Theatre«.

A memorial plaque unveiled in 2001 is a reminder of the five Bernhard world premieres staged at the Landestheater.

THOMAS BERNHARD
1931-1989

Der Ignorant und der Wahnsinnige
1972
Die Macht der Gewohnheit
1974
Am Ziel
1981
Der Theatermacher
1985
Ritter, Dene, Voss
1986

DIE URAUFFÜHRUNGEN DER
SALZBVRGER FEITIPIELE
IM LANDESTHEATER

Gewidmet vom Rotary Club Salzburg 2001

Address Schwarzstrasse 22, A-5020 Salzburg | Public transport Buses no. 1, 3, 4, 5, 6, 21, 22, 25, 27, 160, 170, stops Makartplatz and Theatergasse | Tip In the Scherzhauserfeld-siedlung in Salzburg-Lehen, where Bernhard served an apprenticeship in retail between 1947 and 1949, a street was named after the author in 1996.

100 The Tile murals at the Train Station

Tourism adverts of 1910 reloaded

For a long time, Salzburg's main station was a utilitarian building devoid of charm. However, this all changed recently when several years of reconstruction work revealed some historically significant elements of décor from the turn of the century and »reactivated« them. The eye-catcher in the redesigned entrance hall, now flooded with light, are ten tiled images showing landscape motifs and coats of arms dating from the Golden Age of rail tourism.

In 1909, the images painted on tiles were glued onto the wall at a height of some nine metres/nearly 30 feet, presenting the finest aspects of the city of Salzburg and regions easily accessible from here by train. In 1964, they disappeared behind plaster in the wake of a »modernisation« operation. Following restoration and a new lick of colour, the tile murals started their second life in 2012.

Here you have the blindingly white glacier fields of the Großvenediger peak, over there the deep blue waters of Lake Zell against a backdrop of the Kitzsteinhorn. The mighty Bad Gastein Waterfall is plunging into the depths, and at Hellbrunn Castle, just outside Salzburg, autumnal colours play. The artwork is by Hubert Zwickle, Otto Barth, Hans Purtscher and Hans Wilt, artists who formed part of the circle of influence of the Vienna Workshop, the »Wiener Werkstätte«. Even 100 years after they were made, the messages of tourism still work. You'll notice that when you catch yourself thinking that you really should revisit the Grossglockner, visit Lake Gosau or go for a hike in Matrei's Tauern Valley.

Numerous other decorative Art Nouveau elements and windows modelled on historical designs lend the entrance a turn-of-the-century flair. This symbiosis of conservation and modern architecture was also crowned with success during the renovation of the steel hall above the central platform.

Address Südtiroler Platz 1, A-5020 Salzburg | **Public transport** Bus stop Hauptbahnhof (main train station) | **Tip** The office of Tourismus Salzburg GmbH at the main station is happy to provide visitors with literature and tips (www.salzburg.info). From the Europa Hotel's rooftop cafe diagonally opposite, Mönchsberg and Kapuzinerberg seem close enough to touch; looking north the view extends far into the Flachgau.

101__ The Tomb of Paracelsus
The Alchemist's legacy

»It is only the dose which makes a thing poison« – most people have heard of this quote. It is ascribed to a doctor and natural philosopher, who was not only active in Salzburg but is also seen by some as a key figure in the transition from medieval to modern scientific medicine. Others dismiss him as a mere charlatan. Paracelsus is his name.

Paracelsus was born Philippus Theophrastus Bombastus von Hohenheim in 1493 in Switzerland. His medical training led him through half of Europe. His main interest was treating wounds, miners' diseases and the treatment of syphilis.

Paracelsus observed, tested and proved that water from Gastein's thermal springs, as well as various herbs, had healing powers. His striving for knowledge with an empirical basis brought him in conflict with the established medical fraternity, which was still caught in doctrines from antiquity.

However, Paracelsus' progressive side was twinned with a dark, alchemist one; for instance, he once boasted of having created a homunculus, or artificial human being. This early lateral thinker was practising in Salzburg in 1524/25, when he was forced to leave, apparently due to his sympathies for the suppressed peasant revolt. Fifteen years later he took up renewed residence on the Salzach, where he was to die in 1541. Some 200 years after his death, admirers of Paracelsus had his mortal remains in St. Sebastian's Cemetery exhumed and transferred to an obelisk-shaped tomb monument. The inscription claims that Paracelsus was able to heal leprosy and dropsy – one of the numerous romanticisations of his person. However, the circumstances surrounding his death were apparently bizarre indeed.

An analysis of his bones a few years ago found abnormally high levels of mercury – an indication that he might have poisoned himself while working.

Address St. Sebastian's Cemetery, in the entrance area coming in from Linzer Gasse, A-5020 Salzburg | Opening times Daily April–Oct 9am–6.30pm, Nov–March 9am–4pm | Public transport Buses no. 2, 4, 21, 22, stop Wolf-Dietrich-Strasse | Tip A memorial plaque on house no. 3 in the square is a reminder of the former residence of the medical man. In honour of the man behind the phrase »Beer is a truly divine medicine«, the Stiegl Brewery created the cloudy Paracelsus-Zwickl beer.

102 The Tongue Beards

*Friedrich Hundertwasser's contribution
to Salzburg Modernism*

In the urban landscape of the capital Vienna, Friedensreich Hundertwasser (1928–2000) has a strong presence. He designed the façade of a waste incineration plant using his unmistakable ornaments. He was allowed to implement his ideas about »humane living« in a municipal residential facility and created a museum with no edges or corners. In Salzburg, the artist was given the chance to design only one façade, and even that one was highly controversial.

All the excitement ignited in the early 1980s with the redesign of the Rupertinum, which was supposed to be rebranded from a former seminary for the priesthood and student's lodgings to a museum of modern art. From the outside, the aged building in the heart of the Old Town appeared a little dated, giving the artist the idea to jazz up the façade using simple means. With this in mind, Hundertwasser had decorative elements in the form of shiny gold and silver ceramic tiles attached to the underside of a few windows. With a little imagination you can see tongues in the dangling ceramic surfaces – was that the reason why passersby felt offended, venting their protest in Letters to the Editor? Others felt reminded of carpets hung out to air or for beating.

In any case, the Hundertwasser frames became known as Tongue Beards – and were soon taken down again. Following a cooling-off phase lasting a few years, Hundertwasser's single major artwork for Salzburg was given a second chance in 1987.

Since then, the Tongue Beards have been lending the Rupertinum, today a satellite of the Museum of Modern Art, a cheeky, self-deprecating note. The same can be said of the monumental sculpture by Jorg Immendorff, which the small courtyard in front of the Rupertinum has sheltered for a while now. Showing a band of apes monkeying around, it does actually take away the limelight slightly from the tongue beards.

Address Museum of Modern Art Rupertinum, Wiener Philharmoniker Gasse 9, A-5020 Salzburg, tel. +43 (0)662/842220451, www.museumdermoderne.at | Opening times Museum: Tue–Sun 10am–6pm, Wed 10am–8pm | Public transport Buses no. 1, 4, 8, 22, stop Herbert von Karajan Platz | Tip Alongside top-class exhibitions, the pretty arcaded courtyard is another good reason to take a look at the museum.

103_ The Toy Museum
At last, a wet weather alternative for the little ones

You can look but don't touch! This concept is a thing of the past now, but it took a little while for those in charge of Salzburg's toy museum to realise. Until 2011, the house in Bürgerspitalgasse presented itself as a museum of the classic kind, which might have boasted substantial collections of antique tin soldiers, brass drums, teddy bears, dolls and even toys to play at celebrating Mass with, but had few activity options.

For the museum's young visitors, being allowed only to observe the exhibits lined up tidily and dating from the era of their great grandfathers had limited appeal.

Now it's the other way round. The emphasis is on interaction, discovery and creation – on play if you like. The main attraction is a giant marble run designed by students at the renowned Kuchl woodwork college, which lets the marbles spin across numerous levels, their journey accompanied by melodies.

With the new concept, the sky is the limit for the imagination at the toy museum. Playing with various materials is as much part of the programme as the music sessions. The little visitors can test their motor skills building towers, and their sense of balance on wobbly sofas. Well-equipped tool boxes are a fixture, as is a Carrera racing track.

Striking parallels appear during the changing exhibitions presenting aspects of play in other cultures. You'll learn, for instance, that in China the monkey king has the function of Punch. The few exhibits still behind glass are kept at the eye level of the museum's young guests, so the whole experience doesn't turn into a frustrating one.

Those who find all the action gets too much can retreat to the cosy snug or reading corners, or take a spin on the indoor slide to let off steam. And if everything goes according to plan, the parents can relax at the tea bar. Perfect for a rainy day.

Address Bürgerspitalgasse 2, A-5020 Salzburg, tel. +43 (0)662/620808300, www.salzburgmuseum.at/spielzeugmuseum.html | Opening times Tue– Sun 9am–5pm | Public transport Buses no. 1, 4, 8, 22, stop Herbert-von-Karajan-Platz | Tip Every other week, on a Wednesday, Punch & Judy put in an appearance at Bürgerspitalgasse.

104_ The Triangel

Meeting place for Festival artists and students

»One Peter Simonischek fish soup please!« or »Can I have the Netrebko Salad as a side dish please«. Those taking a seat in the Triangel during Festival time might be excused for disbelieving their ears. Are the names of famous artists being taken in vain here? To the contrary, the cafe-restaurant across from the Festival venues is the secret living room of the singing and acting stars fulfilling engagements here on the banks of the Salzach in July and August. From Anna Netrebko to Patricia Petibon, from Ben Becker to Peter Simonischek – they all feel so at home here that they've lent their names to dishes on the menu.

And the fact that Festival visitors of the calibre of VIP TV host Thomas Gottschalk to Salzburg's adopted son Franz Beckenbauer also frequent the Triangel, can be gauged by the wealth of cards bearing good wishes and personal dedications.

All this doesn't mean that the ambience is snobby or eccentric. Nobody wants to scare away the regulars, so during Festival time, only the 60 seats inside and under the marquees are reserved. On the beer counters beyond the Wiener-Philharmoniker-Gasse, the laidback staff might even bring artists of world renown to join your table. Who, rest assured, display little of the spoilt star attitude.

While you can be sure that the Triangel witnesses people dancing on tables, none of that leaves the restaurant. Which is probably one reason for its popularity.

Another is that, in culinary terms, the cookery team is very strong on regional and organic products, from chanterelle mushrooms from the Lungau to the fish from local waters. Instead of Coke and energy drinks, natural apple juice is served.

When the university term starts up again, the Triangel works as a canteen too, and students populate the tables that just a few weeks previously were crowded with stars.

Address Wiener-Philharmoniker-Gasse 7, A-5020 Salzburg, tel. +43 (0)662/842229, www.triangel-salzburg.co.at | Opening times Mon–Sat 12 noon–midnight, in July and Aug also Sun from 12 noon | Public transport Buses no. 1, 4, 8, 22, stop Herbert-von-Karajan-Platz | Tip If you have some time on your hands before your table reservation, consider visiting the Collegiate church on Universitätsplatz square. The church is a major work by baroque architect Fischer von Erlach.

105 __ The Umbrella Manufacturer

Defeating the famous drizzle

An umbrella! My kingdom for an umbrella! Many a Salzburger and visitor to the city has prayed for one when the dreaded fine drizzle, called »Schnürlregen« (literally 'strings of rain') locally, moves in from the northwest, not unlike the implacable mechanics of a Shake-spearean drama, and starts unleashing its depressing handiwork be-tween the Kapuzinerberg and Mönchsberg hills. And while many people might hurry into a café such as the Tomaselli or the Bazar to bury their faces behind newpapers in the hope that the rain might pass, others grab the bull by the horns, following the motto »There is no such thing as bad weather, only unsuitable clothing«.

A good place to do that is the umbrella manufacturer at Getrei-degasse 22. The »Sonn- und Regenschirmgeschäft Alois Kirchtag«, with its repair service, opened as far back as 1903, but cheap imports from the Far East increasingly turned umbrellas into a sideline. Un-til Andreas Kirchtag, fourth-generation, dared to try a new begin-ning. Umbrellas hand-made from quality materials and as robust as possible, together with an elegant appearance – this turned out to be a successful combination.

The pronounced mushroom shape of the Kirchtag umbrellas is geared towards the requirements of the reputed »capital of drizzle« that is Salzburg. Their backbone is a seamless stick made from high-quality wood, including rosewood, cherry, ash or hickory, one end of which is bent over steam to form a handle. After some fine finishing, a robust framework of rods is added. The materials used for the cover are cotton and parachute silk, and the careful assembly of the indi-vidual components is done by hand. The small company still employs techniques no longer used in the industrialised world of umbrella production. In this way, some 400 umbrellas every year contribute to the success of the family business.

Address Schirmhandel & -manufaktur Kirchtag, Getreidegasse 22, A-5020 Salzburg,
tel. +43 (0)662/841310, www.kirchtag.com | Public transport Buses no. 1, 4, 5, 7, 8, 20, 21,
22, 27, 28, stop Ferdinand-Hanusch-Platz | Tip Museum as bad weather alternative sight-
seeing option – that's a classic in Salzburg too. Not far away, on Museumsplatz 5, the beautifully set-up Haus der Natur natural history museum is well worth a visit.

106___ The Vineyard

Small but perfectly formed: Salzburg's grape harvest

The hedges and walls of Mönchsberg hide not only the odd feudal refuge, but also a culinary speciality: a vineyard yielding high-quality white wine. This draws on a Salzburg tradition from the Middle Ages and early modern times, before climatic changes and perhaps competition from imports resulted in the vines disappearing from the city hills and Salzburg becoming known more as Austria's »beer capital« today.

In 2008, oenophile Salzburgers started an attempt to revive Mönchsberg's wine tradition. The terrain chosen to serve as testing ground was a part of the »Paris-Lodron-Zwinger«, a fortified compound below Richterhöhe. Following in-depth consultation, the decision was made to cultivate Frühroter Veltliner grapes, also called Malvasia. These grapes ripen fairly quickly, which is important because despite the slope's south-easterly orientation and a microclimate enjoying slightly higher temperatures than the surrounding area, the general conditions for viniculture in Salzburg are borderline.

The sweat-inducing work was taken on by Salzburg's scouts who adapted the slope to its new use and have been looking after the vines ever since.

2010 saw the first harvest and winemaking – and lo and behold, the wine, christened »Paris Lodron Zwinger« to reflect its origins, received good reviews.

In 2011, the 538 vines yielded about 500 bottles, plus 30 magnums. Of course, these limited quantities mean that Salzburg's city wine is not exactly widely available.

The main source of distribution of the Frühroter Veltliner, which is described as multifaceted with mineral notes, is through the scouts, with only very small quantities entering the market. The occasional magnum is opened for official receptions, during Festival time for instance.

Address Mönchsberg 16, near Richterhöhe, A-5020 Salzburg | Public transport Buses no. 1, 4, 8, 22, stop Herbert-von-Karajan-Platz, 20 minutes on foot via Toscanini-Hof and Clemens-Holzmeister-Stiege; or via Mönchsbergaufzug elevator from Mönchsbergaufzug bus stop, about 15 minutes on foot across Mönchsberg | Tip The Richterhöhe offers good views of Salzburg's only vineyard. Visitors wanting to purchase a bottle of »Paris Lodron Zwinger« can try their luck at the Pfadfinderhaus scout's HQ (Fürstenallee 45), Spirituosen Sporer (Getreidegasse 39) or at the Feinkost Kölbl deli (Theatergasse 2). The wine list of the artHOTEL Blaue Gans sometimes features this exotic local beverage.

107__The Wild Man Fountain
An archaic sight in the Festival zone

Salzburg is not exactly short of lavish water features and magnificent fountains. And in recent times, with the Wilder-Mann or Fish-market Fountain on Max-Reinhardt-Platz square, the city fountain most shrouded in legend has been made resplendent once again. The main eye-catcher is the fountain figure, of the Wild Man variety, sporting a long beard, rough skin, fingers as thin as twigs and a head covered in leaves. In his right-hand, he is wielding a cudgel or tree trunk torn from the soil, in his left the city's coat of arms. On its columned pedestal, the figure appears archaic and imposing. Deeply rooted in the folklore of many Central European cultures, »Wild Men« stood for the threat of nature as well as the untamed side of humankind.

Exact interpretations are lost in the mists of time, but what is certain is that Salzburg's Wild Man was created around 1620. The sculpture worked from copper sheet – originally sporting colourful paint – became the companion and guard of the Fishmarket Fountain, one of the few watering holes in Salzburg to be erected by its citizens. The city's coat-of-arms in his left hand is an indication of the fact that the Wild Man is also credited with powers of guardianship.

The copper-green fellow has travelled extensively. Every time the fish market moved, he too had to move – until the construction of the Festival venue in 1926.

At the time, the fish market was moved to the banks of the Salzach, while the fountain came to its last station to date on the edge of the Furtwängler Garden. The marble fish tanks were taken off and replaced by a simple pond. However, there are no more fish swimming around at the feet of the Wild Man for him to order around like Neptune. Maybe that's why he is looking a bit grim. But who knows, his sight might provide inspiration to the odd actor at Festival HQ opposite…

Address Max Reinhardt Platz, A-5020 Salzburg | Public transport Buses no. 1, 4, 8, 22, stop Herbert-von-Karajan-Platz | Tip The Old Town area alone boasts 14 drinking water fountains for visitors to slake their thirst. There's even an online brochure at www.stadt-salzburg.at/pdf/trinkbrunnen_der_stadt_salzburg.pdf.

108__ The Witches Tower Memorial Plaque

A dark chapter in Salzburg's judicial history

A commemorative plaque, a sign with a witch on her broom, a mosaic on a house wall with the silhouette of a woman burning at the stake – the corner of Paris-Lodron-Strasse and Wolf-Dietrich-Strasse provides a number of clues to a sombre chapter of judicial history. This is where the witches tower stood up to a bomb attack in 1944. It took its name from the time around 1680, when a witch-hunt hysteria was sweeping Salzburg.

It had its roots in the social conflicts of the second half of the 17th century. Beggars roamed the country and petty crime was on the rise. The Catholic authorities did not look too kindly on these uncontrollable elements. And suddenly, after a hailstorm and one or two cows found dead, somebody started circulating the rumour that they had joined forces with the devil under the leadership of »Magician Jackl«, poisoning water, cattle and the harvest. People were arrested, and under torture they would accuse somebody they knew, who in turn would accuse a family, turning an isolated case into an avalanche.

As the cells were overflowing in the city hall, an old tower of the fortified wall was adapted as a prison for suspects from all over the country. One of the stories surrounding this place of horror is that »witches« were kept prisoners in hanging vats to stop their feet touching the ground and them evaporating into thin air. The ensuing witch-hunts are considered to have been the cruellest in the territory of what is now Austria. Up to 1690, 138 accused were put to death by strangling, decapitation and burning.

Historians have pieced together, using the available court documents, that four fifths were male, two thirds under 21 years old, and the youngest victim ten years old. Nearly all came from the lower rungs of society. Jackl was never heard from again.

Address Paris-Lodron-Strasse 16/Wolf-Dietrich-Strasse 19, A-5020 Salzburg | Public transport Buses no. 2, 4, 21, 22, stop Wolf-Dietrich-Straße | Tip Every last Friday of the month tourist guide Sabine Rath offers a special tour to the dark places of Salzburg's history (tel. +43 (0)664/2016492, www.tourguide-salzburg.com).

109__ The Devil's Ditch

Where crossbowmen like to tuck into their ribs

In fact, the devil didn't have any hand in creating the Teufelsgraben on Lake Obertrum – that was done by erosion and other natural forces. A nature trail familiarises visitors with the geology as well as the flora and fauna of this forested gorge, leading past the Wildkar waterfall to two mills that have been revitalized in the wake of the »Teufelsgraben« eco-cultural project: a marble mill and a flour mill.

The passing on of knowledge and old traditions is highly valued in the region, as shown by the example of the crossbowmen. Hermann Rosenstatter, organic farmer and owner of the Schiessentobel hostelry, set up a crossbow shooting range in his farmyard as far back as the 1980s, to provide the »Seehamer Stachelschützen« with a home for their archery competitions.

Alongside the Salzburg regional championships, a good number of anniversary, wedding and honorary shooting events are staged here, most of them combined with a sociable rib feast. A »master bowman« ensures safety, while every archer who hits the target is given his disc as a souvenir. From groups of 12 upwards, visitors are given the opportunity to get more closely acquainted with this ancient skill.

At the nearby Paulsepplgut farm, Johann Steiner, regional champion several times over, runs a crossbow workshop as a sideline. Johann taught himself the craft and is constantly developing it, using the finest nutwoods for his crossbows.

In the Brechelbad Museum right next door, visitors can get an idea of how flax was transformed into linen until the middle of the last century.

In terms of cultural history, the highlight in the Teufelsgraben is the Rohrmoosmühle mill, where organic farmers from the lake country around Trum have their cereals ground the traditional way. The miller himself will guide you through the restored mill with its clattering workings.

Address One possible entrance is at the organic Bio Hotel Schiessentobel, Schiessentobel 1, A-5164 Seeham (Matzing), www.teufelsgraben.at | Access Take the exit Salzburg Nord in the direction of Obertrum | Tip The Teufelsgraben Loop can be walked in 1.5 kilometre/ just under one mile and 2.5 kilometre/1.5 miles routes. Guided walks are organised by the Tourismusverband Seeham tourism association (tel. +43 (0)6217/5493).

110_ The Wenger Moor
Back to the Ice Ages

You just know that they are flitting about somewhere out there, the kingfishers, the corncrakes, the red-backed shrikes, the common snipes and lapwings and all the others.

The Wenger Moor, outside the gates of Salzburg, is a paradise for birds, with plenty of action from spring to autumn – in ornithological terms anyway. Little wonder, as the nature reserve spanning 300 hectares on the northwestern banks of Lake Waller offers our feathered friends excellent breeding conditions and a ready supply of food to their taste. The same holds true for amphibians and insects by the way.

This mosaic of landscapes extending between the communities of Seekirchen, Kostendorf and Neumarkt, comprises high and lower moors, forested islets, ponds with deadwood, meandering rivulets, marshy meadows and a reed-fringed riverine zone. The driving force behind this landscape was an arm of the Salzach Glacier, which melted 12,000 years ago leaving interim areas between water and land as enchanting as they are vulnerable.

Since the ecological stabilisation of Lake Waller, nature lovers too can enjoy it once more. A good starting point is a circular trail beginning at the small village of Weng and offering fine views from an observation tower.

Another option is to head into the Wenger Moor from Seekirchen in the south or Neumarkt at the northern end of the lake. Display panels provide information on the various habitats and their inhabitants, but some parts of the moor are out of bounds to visitors – leaving space for rare birds to breed here. To get on their trail simply requires a pair of binoculars and a degree of patience.

Or you can leave the encounters to chance, and you'll still witness many of the little wonders of nature: a meadow of wild flowers and butterflies fluttering, a concert of frogs from a brackish pond, or simply dewdrops in the grass.

Address Between A-5201 Seekirchen, A-5203 Weng and A-5202 Neumarkt am Waller-see | **Public transport** Take the S 2 from Salzburg in one of the three villages; you can take your bike with you | Anfahrt A 1 Richtung Linz / Wien, exit 281-Wallersee, then feel your way towards the Wenger Moor via the B 1, L 102 and L 238 in a northerly direction | **Tip** Our recommendation: guided hikes through the moors with farmer and nature guide Josef Wengler (tel. +43 (0)6216 / 6370). Don't miss the fish specialities in Restaurant Winkler on the coast road 33 (Neumarkt am Wallersee).

111__ The Motorway Border Crossing

From the bottleneck of Europe to the »non place«

»Munich – Salzburg motorway: the tailback at the entrance to the Walserberg border crossing has swollen to 60 kilometres/37 miles. Estimated waiting time for entering Austria: two hours.« It's not so long ago that distressing news of this kind formed part of a dreaded routine for stressed German holidaymakers on their pilgrimage south. And on the way back, the convoys would be greeted by the exact same scenario. That's all in the past now, as from 1 April 1998 the Schengen Agreement has spelled free transit at what used to be Europe's biggest border crossing.

The Großer Walserberg bottleneck, once infamous through its frequent appearance on traffic news, has over time transformed itself into a »non-place«. Most customs buildings fell victim to the metamorphosis, while the bridge constructed for the 1972 Summer Olympic Games in Munich is also no longer standing. Getting out of the car to buy the vignette tax disc for Austria's motorways, all you'll see today is a chunky hotel going by the name of »Servus Europa«.

Petrol stations, shops and a restaurant also provide a break from the journey. Otherwise, it's concrete, asphalt and trucks waiting to be dispatched, surrounded by roaring engines of the kind you'd expect during a Formula 1 warm-up.

What has remained is a rich depository of stories. Albin Kühnel, the former head of the German Customs office on Walserberg, experienced births and deaths here. One event in particular stayed in his mind: a German man asked him whether a dowry was taxable. He had married an Austrian girl who brought a wine cellar into the marriage. Kühnel had to tell him that alcohol did not fall under the category of duty-free wedding goods. To which the man replied: »If I'd known that I wouldn't have got married.«

Address A-5071 Wals near Salzburg | Access A1 from the east / A8 coming from
Germany | Tip Leave the motorway for Wals-Siezenheim near Salzburg and visit the
exhibition on the Roman palatial villa of Loig in the local »Bachschmiede« museum.

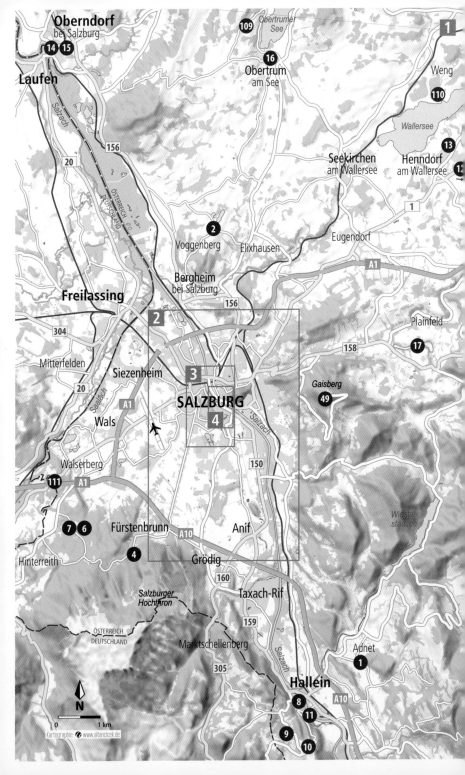

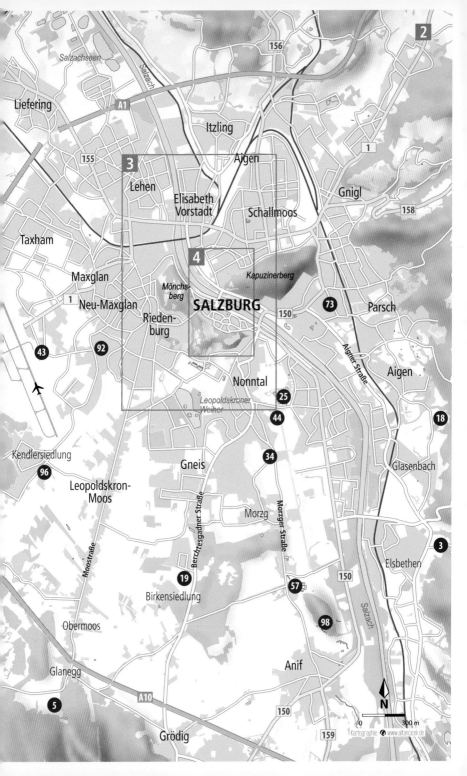

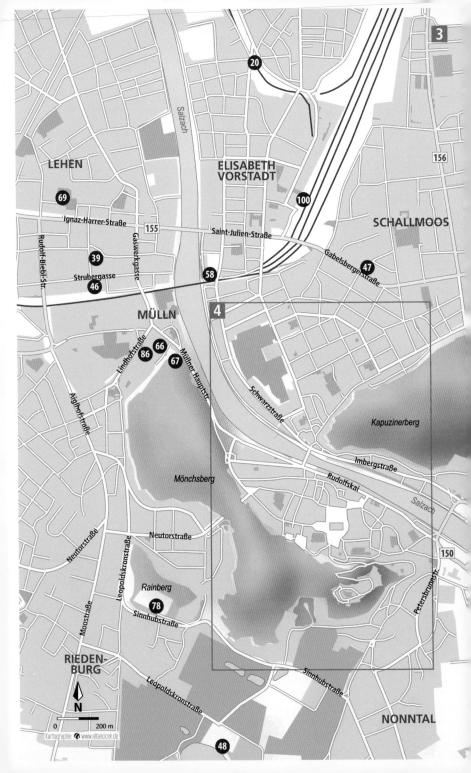

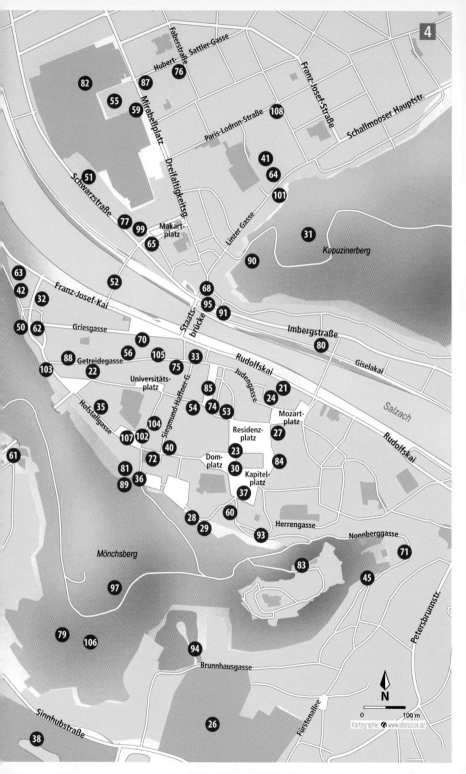

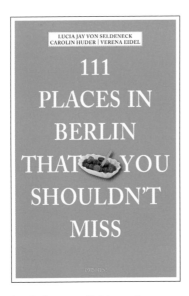

Lucia Jay von Seldeneck,
Carolin Huder, Verena Eidel
**111 PLACES IN BERLIN
THAT YOU SHOULDN'T MISS**
ISBN 978-3-95451-208-9

Berlin is big. Huge. No one can ever say: I've done Berlin!
But it is worth exploring the city over an over again.
This book shows you the way to 111 little-known, strange
and fascinating places.
How do you get to the ghost rail station in Siemensstadt?
How much does it cost to stay in the Princess's Room
in an old socialist tower block in Marzahn?
And where in Berlin will you meet the boatmen's pastor?
These 111 discoveries are resonant with pictures and stories,
places with an individual atmosphere. This is Berlin for the
curious, for the explorer off the beaten track.

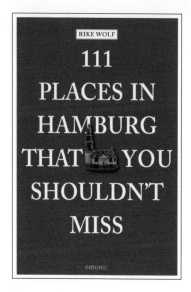

Rike Wolf
**111 PLACES IN HAMBURG
THAT YOU SHOULDN'T MISS**
ISBN 978-3-95451-234-8

Have you ever stood on a square that doesn't officially exist?
Do you know the ancient chest where you can take
a shuddering look at the bones of famous pirate Störtebeker?
And where can you hear a thousand stories about the port
of Hamburg?
This book answers these and other questions –
discover 111 fascinating, eccentric and unusual places.

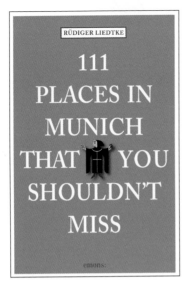

Rüdiger Liedtke
111 PLACES IN MUNICH
THAT YOU SHOULDN'T MISS
ISBN 978-3-95451-222-5

Have you ever had hallucinations in Fröttmaning?
Do you know about the theater canteen where you
can spend a fabulous evening?
Where can you see 500 living reptiles in one place?
And do you know where you can be close enough
to Thomas Mann's brown bear to touch it?
This book tells untold tales and takes even long-time
residents of Munich to places that will astound them.